THE TRIAL OF
RICHARD III

THE TRIAL OF
RICHARD III

Richard Drewett and Mark Redhead

ALAN SUTTON

First published in the United Kingdom in 1984
Alan Sutton Publishing Limited, Brunswick Road, Gloucester

First published in the United States of America in 1990
Alan Sutton Publishing Inc., Wolfeboro Falls, NH 03896–0840

First published 1984
Reprinted 1985, 1987, 1990

British Library Cataloguing in Publication Data

Drewett, Richard
    The trial of Richard III.
    1. Richard III, *King of England*
    I. Title II. Redhead, Mark
    942.04'6'0924   DA260

    ISBN 0–86299–198–6

Library of Congress Cataloging-in-Publication Data

Drewett, Richard
    The trial of Richard III / Richard Drewett and Mark Redhead.
        p.   cm.
    ISBN 0–86299–198–6 : $11.00
    1. Richard III, King of England, 1452–1485.   2. Great Britain –
History – Richard III, 1483–1485.   3. Great Britain – Kings and rulers
– Biography.   4. Mock trials.   I. Redhead, Mark.   II. Title.
    [DA260.D73   1989]
    942.04'6'092–dc20
    [B]
                                                            89–36155
                                                            CIP

Typesetting and orgination by
Alan Sutton Publishing Limited.
Printed in Great Britain.

THE AUTHORS

RICHARD DREWETT, who devised and produced *The Trial of Richard III*, started work as a journalist writing radio scripts in his spare time. His career as a television producer began with *Late Night Line Up* for BBC2 in 1964. Since then he has worked for the BBC, ITV, German and Spanish television, and co-produced a feature film – *F for Fake* with Orson Welles. He is currently Head of Special Programmes for London Weekend Television.

MARK REDHEAD, the Associate Producer of *The Trial of Richard III*, studied English at Newcastle University. He worked as a reporter on a provincial newspaper before joining the Special Programmes Department of London Weekend Television as a researcher in 1982.

TELEVISION PRODUCTION CREDITS

Senior Cameraman	:	DAVE TAYLOR
Vision Controller	:	FRANK PARKER
Vision Mixer	:	BARBARA HICKS
Videotape Editor	:	GRAHAM SISSONS
Floor Manager	:	WALLY KING
Stage Manager	:	JANE DENHOLM
Graphics	:	CHRIS SHARP
Make Up	:	SANDY MACFARLANE
Costume Design	:	SUE THOMSON
Production Assistant	:	JULIA WEEDON
Production Manager	:	ROGER ALLSOPP
Sound Supervisor	:	MIKE FAIRMAN
Lighting Director	:	BRYAN LOVE
Design	:	BRYAN BAGGE
Researcher	:	KERRY PLATMAN
Associate Producer	:	MARK REDHEAD
Devised and Produced by	:	RICHARD DREWETT
Directed by	:	GRAHAM C. WILLIAMS

CONTENTS

THE
IDEA

In February 1980, while attending a London Weekend programme planning conference, I found myself at dinner next to the company's new Director of Corporate Affairs, Jeremy Potter. It was the first time we had talked at length, and he soon launched into a subject which I was to discover was of more than passing interest to him – the life and character of Richard III. I learned then of the existence of the Richard III Society, of which he is Chairman – a group of enthusiasts who devote a great deal of time and energy to writing, researching, and discussing all aspects of the history of the King and his times, as well as working as an efficient public relations organisation for their hero. Equipped as I was with only a smattering of knowledge of the period and a vivid picture of Laurence Olivier as Richard, this was a fairly one-sided conversation.

Warming to his theme, Jeremy Potter explained that many believed Richard's character and name had been blackened by the Tudors and Thomas More, caricatured by Shakespeare and misrepresented by history ever since. His record before he became King was as an excellent and fair administrator in the North. There was no justification for condemning him for the murder of his nephews. For every shred of evidence, there were alternative explanations and other probable culprits.

That evening the germ of an idea began to form. There is, of course, nothing like a good murder mystery, and although this one has been the subject of countless books, novels and many television programmes, these had all ended with a question mark, or come down on one side or the other depending on the subjective attitude of the authors or producers. But what about a trial? Not simply an exploration of the arguments, or a presentation of one point of view, but a trial by the rules of British justice, with the arguments presented by barristers and expert witnesses before a judge and jury, and finally, a verdict on Richard's guilt or innocence of the murder of the Princes in the Tower. It was a simple concept but one fraught with immense problems. Apart from the fact that it would have only minority appeal, there was simply not the screen time available to do justice to such a programme in the competitive world of ITV. So a few notes went onto a file, and, though from time to time I met Jeremy Potter and the subject was mentioned, it remained a talking point and nothing more.

Then in November 1982 Channel Four started transmission with a deliberate policy to transmit programmes that broke away from the subject and scheduling limitations of the main commercial channel. With the 500th anniversary of Richard III's coronation due in July 1983 the time seemed right, and a simple proposal was sent to Channel Four in January of that year. The reaction was refreshingly swift and positive. The programme was commissioned, and an unformed idea suddenly became a project.

The Special Programmes Department at London Weekend Television sets out to make entertaining talk and documentary programmes with a broad appeal. Though experienced in bringing the best out of the famous and the unknown alike, this was our first departure into the historical field. There was a great deal of research to be done, and the process of translating it into a programme had still to be worked out. The idea seemed simple enough, but a surprising number of people found it hard to grasp what we were up to. 'Who's writing the script?' 'Who's playing the part of Richard?' were questions asked time and time again.

To start the production process I asked Mark Redhead, who had joined the department direct from a career in journalism, and had worked on a number of unscripted talk-based programmes, to join me as Associate Producer and chief editorial mind on the project. He grasped the concept with gratifying ease, and to him must go a large part of any credit due for the final programme. Later he was joined by a researcher, Kerry Platman, and, two months before the actual recording, our ranks were strengthened by the director Graham Williams, who had the unenviable task of tailoring the editorial demands of the programme to the practical and technical limitations of a television studio. My assistant throughout the project was Claire Nye.

What follows is a description of the process that began with a first editorial meeting in July 1983, and resulted in the recording of the Trial on the afternoon and evening of 21st February 1984. Inevitably it relies on Mark Redhead's recollections and descriptions of the detailed work he was responsible for. The full transcript of the Trial is printed together with some additional editorial notes.

The production proved a fascinating exercise for us all – not only from the aspect of the historical questions that had to be explored, but in the way that it allowed us an insight into the workings of the British legal system.

RICHARD DREWETT
July 1984

THE
MAKING OF
THE TRIAL

THE SOURCES

The controversy that surrounds the last Plantagenet king is not a dry and dusty historical debate, but a live issue, one that arouses passions as fierce as those that rage in contemporary politics. This was made abundantly clear by the thick file of press cuttings on Richard III. Ordered on impulse, as though it was a programme on a modern political figure that was being made and not one on a late-fifteenth century king, the cuttings went back to the early 1950s. They included running debates conducted in the letters' pages of the *Daily Telegraph* and *The Times*, vitriolic book reviews, news stories and feature articles explaining the latest developments in the longest running controversy in English history.

A *Daily Telegraph* report from 1955 captured the hot-blooded spirit of the argument. The article noted that a society, the Friends of Richard III Inc., had been formed in America to combat the traditional view of the last Plantagenet king. The actresses Helen Hayes and Tallulah Bankhead were among the 75 founding members. Miss Bankhead had been unable to attend the New York launch, but sent a telegram which read 'Libelled by history, fouled by legend, Richard III must be whitewashed and his bones find their deserved crypt in the Abbey. Let us have no shilly-shallying.' On the anti-Richard side it seemed that feelings ran equally high. One correspondent writing to the editor of *The Times* snorted that Richard's apologists simply did not understand the logical conclusion of their arguments which attacked the Tudors for blackening the name of their hero. 'If he (Richard) had been loyal to the legitimate king, his nephew Edward V, the Tudors would have had no opportunity of claiming the throne at all, still less of launching their propaganda against him.' As we read such words the realisation began to dawn that we had in our hands an ancient, but still extremely hot, potato. It was inevitable

that the trial would leave one side aggrieved. A philosophical acceptance of this fact and a neutral view of the subject were the attitudes that
had to be adopted.

Books on Richard III range from the childishly superficial to works of
massively-detailed scholarship. Two books emerged as useful in map-
ping out the general topography of the subject from the two opposing
broadly guilty and not guilty vantage points: Charles Ross's *Richard III*
and Paul Murray Kendall's *King Richard the Third*. Though these and
other works on the subject were useful, it was clear that reliance would
have to be placed on the documentary material of the period for the
construction of the cases for and against King Richard. Contrary to
expectations, his brief reign is reasonably well documented; the two
most important texts being the *Second Continuation of the Croyland
Chronicle* written in Croyland Abbey, Lincolnshire, and *The Usurpation of
Richard III* by Dominic Mancini. These two works provided the bulk of
the evidence discussed in the trial and much argument was to centre
around their meaning and reliability.

The most important and comprehensive account of the time is the
Croyland Chronicle, a political memoir covering the period from 1459 to
1486. According to its author, it was written in ten days in April 1486.
The identity of this author is uncertain; Bishop John Russell, Richard's
own Chancellor, is the most popular candidate. Whoever it was, his
knowledge of events at the centre of power in England in Richard's
reign suggests he was a member of the king's council. The tenor of the
account is hostile to Richard and the author clearly believes that Richard
should not have taken the throne from his nephew, the young King
Edward V. The chronicler mentions the death of the Princes twice in his
story. Once when discussing the rebellion which took place against
Richard in the autumn of 1483 he writes, 'A rumour was spread that the
sons of King Edward before named had died, but it was uncertain
how . . .'. Later he quotes the verses of 'a certain poet' on the three King
Richards of England. On Richard III the verses read:

> 'Edward's vast hoards of wealth consumed, the Third
> Was not content there with, but must destroy
> His brother's progeny . . .'

*De Occupatione Regni Anglie per Riccardum Tercium, The Usurpation of
Richard III*, by Dominic Mancini is a remarkably vivid and apparently
objective account of events up until June 1483 when its author left
England to return to France. Mancini wrote his work for Angelo Cato,

the Archbishop of Vienne, in December of the same year. Apparently speaking little English, he depended for his information on other Italians in London and on such Italian speakers as the young King Edward V's physician, Dr. John Argentine. As Mancini says in his introduction, the account is not complete in all its details, 'rather shall it resemble the effigy of a man which lacks some of the limbs, and yet a beholder delineates for himself a man's Form.' As with the *Croyland Chronicle*, it was clear that there would be much argument about the evidence provided by Mancini for, at one point, he writes of 'the Duke of Gloucester, who shortly after destroyed Edward's children, and then claimed for himself the throne,' but later, when reporting suspicions that the young King Edward had been killed, he writes, 'Whether, however, he had been done away with and by what manner of death, so far I have not at all discovered.'

Other sources were also available: letters; including some from the City of York archives; official documents including Parliamentary Rolls; three London Chronicles and later histories from the Tudor period such as those written by Sir Thomas More, Philippe de Commynes, John Rous and Polydore Vergil. Though none of these documents provided conclusive cast-iron proof of Richard's guilt or innocence, they offered much material from which both the defence and the prosecution could construct detailed cases. It was beyond the scope of the programme for the research team to pore over the original documents. Fortunately this was unnecessary for the most important texts are readily accessible in translation and in such collections as *English Historical Documents 1327–1485*, edited by Professor A.R. Myers and published in 1969, and Alison Hanham's *Richard III and his Early Historians*, published in 1975. Questions of scholastic interpretation would be a matter for the expert witnesses.

Lord Elwyn-Jones of Llanelli and Newham, the judge

THE LAW

To undertake the trial of a king demanded barristers of the highest calibre, Queen's Counsel at the peak of their professional careers. After some enquiries in the world of criminal advocacy, two of the country's leading QCs were approached. Both immediately showed great enthusiasm for tackling such an unusual case, but before giving a firm commitment they had to apply to their profession's ruling body, the Bar Council, for permission to appear. Satisfied that the appearance of the two would not contravene the profession's rules forbidding advertising, the Bar Council promptly gave its permission with the rider that the barristers should be anonymous and should not wear wigs; it was agreed, however, that they could wear plain black gowns. From a television point of view the wigless state of the barristers came as something of a disappointment. Some members of the production team feared that the bare heads would detract from the authentic court-room atmosphere. In the event, the missing detail was of no consequence. Two top flight barristers in action could not be mistaken for any other class of human being and, by the same token, putting a wig on an actor's head does not transform him into a silk. That the barristers were appearing simply out of an interest in the case was demonstrated by the fact that they both requested their fees be paid to charity.

Having secured the services of the QCs, attention was turned next to the judge. A sitting judge would not be allowed to take part, but after consultations with the QCs one ideal candidate for the task emerged. Lord Elwyn-Jones of Llanelli and Newham was well qualified: he had read history at Cambridge; been a successful QC in England and Wales; acted as a prosecutor at one of the most remarkable trials of the century, the war crimes trial at Nuremburg; sat as a Recorder of Cardiff; served as a Member of Parliament; and, at the culmination of his political and legal careers, had been Attorney General and then the head of the country's judiciary from 1974–1979 as Lord Chancellor in the Wilson and Callaghan Labour governments. He still presents the opposition's case in the House of Lords and sits from time to time as a Lord of Appeal in the nation's highest court. In addition to this wealth of experience, Lord Elwyn-Jones is blessed with an informal manner, considerable patience and courtesy and a splendid Welsh turn of phrase. Like the two barristers,

Lord Elwyn-Jones agreed to take part in the programme. Unlike them he was not governed by rules of anonymity, though, in common with them, he did not wear a wig and appeared in a simple black silk gown.

In November the production team, the two barristers and Lord Elwyn-Jones met to establish the rules of the trial. It was agreed by everyone, including the defence counsel, that the burden of proof should lie with the prosecution whilst the standard of proof should be, as in civil cases, that of the balance of probability, instead of proof beyond reasonable doubt which is the usual requirement in the criminal courts. This was appropriate since the alleged murder of the Princes had taken place so long ago as to make certainty unachievable. The witnesses would have to present the facts as they emerged from the documentary records of the time. Lord Elwyn-Jones argued that the swearing of an oath before a serious but pretend court would not be appropriate and he doubted whether the integrity of the witnesses would be in contention. The barristers agreed and the witnesses were not sworn. It was at this meeting that Lord Elwyn-Jones also came up with the formula to describe the nature of the proceedings. 'As the great historian Lord Acton wrote, "History is a judgement seat" and Richard III is to be tried before the bar of history,' he declared; subsequently employing the same ringing words in his address to the jury. It was also at this meeting that the barristers chose the surnames they would use to preserve their anonymity during the trial. The counsel for the prosecution decided to use his mother's maiden name of Russell and the defence counsel chose Dillon, a treasured family name.

Though equally superb advocates, the two men had markedly different styles. This, it was anticipated, would make a fascinating contrast in the court-room. Mr Russell, a lean and wiry bespectacled figure, had the reputation of being a meticulous and thoughtful builder of cases, rather than an advocate given to spectacular rhetorical devices. He devoted a great amount of time to getting to know the subject, worrying each issue like the proverbial terrier until he felt he had grasped it. The research team spent many evenings in his chambers fielding questions and hammering out the background. The defence counsel, by contrast, had a reputation as a more virtuoso advocate. Dark and hawkishly handsome, his command of language and sense of timing were legendary. These talents were erected on the firm foundation of an acute legal mind. The researchers met with Mr Dillon less frequently than with Mr Russell, partly because he was often busy with cases in distant parts of the country and partly because it seemed he preferred to play his cards close to his chest. So much so that during the trial he made at least one telling point that had not emerged in discussions with any of the witnesses, the production team or even from the literature on the period.

The working arrangement which had been devised between the QC and the editorial team was rather like that between barristers and solicitors in more orthodox court cases. The researchers would marshall the witnesses and set out the evidence from which the barristers would construct their cases. The barristers were supplied with copies of all the relevant contemporary and near-contemporary documents, such as Croyland and Mancini, with assessments of their value and significance. They also received background dossiers on the leading characters in the drama. As the barristers began to develop their cases, they requested briefs on questions that were puzzling them, such as the taking of sanctuary in the fifteenth century, the power of parliament at the time, the consequences of attainder and the autumn rebellion of 1483. Rather than simply dropping the barristers into the controversy, however, the researchers did attempt at a very early stage to set out for them the broad lines of the cases for and against Richard III, from which they could select the particular arguments they wanted to pursue.

THE WITNESSES

No matter what the researchers could offer by way of background it was all waste paper unless there were witnesses who were capable of going into court and giving evidence; people not only with expertise in the field, but with the confidence and ability to stand up in public and express their views in front of television cameras and to defend those positions under cross-examination by two eminent barristers. Theoretically ideal cases for both sides could have been designed and then drilled into a group of intelligent performers. Apart from the danger of these puppets being rapidly exposed by the QCs, it was contrary to the spirit of the project. It was not the job of the programme makers to put words into the witnesses' mouths, but to support the barrister in bringing out as clearly as possible the points the real experts had to make.

It was to the community of academic historians that the research team had turned for the potential prosecution witnesses. The opening sally was somewhat discouraging, for by chance the first professional historian approached was the distinguished Tudor expert Professor Geoffrey Elton. Professor Elton has taken an interest in Richard III over the years, but he refused to have anything to do with the programme on the grounds that, as far as he and most historians were concerned, Richard III was a gangster who had killed the Princes, and a trial, no matter what its outcome, would only serve to revive the debate. It became clear that in some sense Professor Elton was right, few academic historians of the period devote much of their time to raking over the evidence surrounding the deaths of the Princes. Most concentrate their efforts on more general constitutional questions, and the study of patronage and affinity, which reveals the nitty gritty of political struggle.

Nevertheless most of the historians approached offered encouragement and showed great interest in the project. Among the authorities who took the time and trouble to talk to the researchers were: Professor Ralph Griffiths of University College, Swansea, Professor Barry Dobson of York University, Dr Colin Richmond of Warwick University, Dr Rosemary Horrox of Cambridge University Extramural Department, Professor David Morgan of University College, London, Dr Bertram Woolf of Exeter University, Dr A.L. Rowse of All Souls Oxford, and Dr

THE STAGING

It was thought that an appropriate historical location might provide an atmospheric setting for the trial. Three locations in London appeared suitable: The Guildhall in the City, Crosby Hall in Chelsea and the Tower of London itself. The Guildhall, where the Duke of Buckingham had presented Richard's claim to the throne to the City, had also been the location of a number of aristocratic trials, particularly during the Tudor period. Unfortunately, though it was built between 1411 and 1439, the Guildhall was devastated by the Great Fire of 1666 and again by the Blitz in 1940 and little of the original medieval building remains to be seen. It still retains a grand atmosphere, but it was clear that the modern statues of such distinguished twentieth century figures as Sir Winston Churchill would present problems.

Crosby Hall in Cheyne Walk, Chelsea seemed a better prospect. It had formerly stood in Bishopsgate in the City and had been Richard's first lodging in London on his arrival in 1483. In 1908 it was dismantled and by some curious irony was rebuilt in the garden of what was once Sir Thomas More's home in Chelsea. A superb hammer-beam roofed building, it began to seem a less practical idea when it was discovered the extent to which the constant rumble of traffic along the Embankment disturbs its peace. According to its warden, a concert of medieval music which was made in the building for Channel Four had to be recorded between two and four in the morning to escape the noise. Finally the possibility of using the Tower of London was investigated. For the purposes of the trial only those buildings which had been standing at the time of Richard III were suitable and of those only the White Tower was large enough. Not unreasonably the authorities could not clear the White Tower as it houses one of the world's leading collections of armoury and is a major tourist attraction.

In the event it was realised that the idea of a historical setting for the trial had been a red herring and the failure to find such a location was fortunate. The logic of a modern trial demanded a court-room in the style used today. The designer, Bryan Bagge, was asked to provide such a setting. After much research he finally designed a replica of Court Number Four at the Old Bailey, one of the original grand panelled Victorian court-rooms. Such an enclosed space presented the director,

A scene from the trial as seen on television . . .

. . . and a long-shot showing the cameras and the sliding panels built
into the replica court-room

Graham Williams, with the problem of how to shoot the programme. His solution was to hide four cameras behind panels which slid back when the cameras were needed and closed again when they were not in use. Though theoretically simple, this device demanded skilful juggling to ensure that no cameras appeared in shot. An unfamiliar historical setting might have proved a distraction to the lawyers. Locating the trial in a court-room made them feel at home. So accurate was the set that after the trial the prosecuting counsel remarked 'I have appeared in Court Number Four literally hundreds of times so I did not suffer from any nerves at all. In fact, on one occasion I sat down after being on my feet for a long time and realised "I'm in a television studio".'

The bones were found in 1674 underneath a stone staircase in a building (now demolished) which adjoined this part of the Tower

THE BONES

One of the most intriguing and controversial aspects of the case is the discovery of the bones of two children in the Tower of London in 1674. The bones were declared to be those of the Princes and placed in a Wren urn inscribed to that effect in Westminster Abbey. In 1933 they were disinterred and examined by the then Keeper of Muniments at the Abbey, Mr Lawrence Tanner and the President of the Anatomical Society of Great Britain, Professor W. Wright. They concluded from their examination that the story of the deaths of the Princes as told by More was substantially true. In Professor Wright's judgement the ages of the two children (the elder appeared to be between twelve and thirteen and the younger between nine and eleven) were consistent with the ages of the two princes in the late summer of 1483 (Edward is estimated to have been about twelve years nine months and Richard almost ten in August 1483). In addition Professor Wright said there was evidence of a family relationship in the jaws and bones of the two children. He also said that a red stain across the facial bones of the elder child was a blood stain resulting from suffocation. Tanner and Wright had introduced an unexpectedly emotional note in a paper written for presentation to the learned Society of Antiquaries. They conclude their report: 'While the bones of Richard III have long since disappeared, trampled into the common clay, those of the Princes, freed from all undignified associations, rest secure in the company of those of their mighty ancestors at the very heart of the national shrine.'

Since 1934, when the paper was published, a number of experts have considered the findings and cast doubt upon its conclusions. Doubts have been expressed about the dating of the teeth and bones and the staining of the skull as a result of suffocation. In view of this apparent dissatisfaction with the 1933 examination a number of experts were approached to see what could be learnt from the bones today. It became clear that fifty years of research into the development of bones and teeth would make it possible to make a more accurate assessment of the age of the two children at death. In addition, microscopic tests to determine the age of bones have been developed at Sheffield University's Department of Pre-History and Archaeology by Professor Keith Branigan. Professor Branigan also said that his department had devised tests of bones for determining gender. There seems little prospect of developing tests to determine the cause of death.

Since 1933, major advances have been made in the dating of archaeological material by the Carbon 14 method. The method relies upon the presence of minute quantities of radio-active carbon in ordinary organic material. In common with all radio-active materials, Carbon 14 decays over a period of time, and the pattern of decay can reveal the age of an object. But scientists at the Atomic Energy Authority laboratory at Harwell in Oxfordshire told us that a piece of bone could be dated only to an accuracy of plus or minus eighty years. Thus, theoretically, a result which placed them in the Roman period would dismiss them from the late Middle Ages, but a result which placed them in the 1480's would not prove that they were murdered in Richard's reign. In fact, the result of a Carbon 14 test could be completely misleading. The bones were found in the seventeenth century at the time when the widespread burning of fossil fuels began. According to the Harwell experts, Carbon 14 from those fuels could find its way into the bones of a seventeenth-century child and give a wildly distorted reading. In addition, we were warned that, though it is possible to conduct tests with small pieces of bone, a reasonably accurate test would require about six grams of carbon and about one kilogram, 'a good leg bone', is required to produce this amount, the bone being destroyed in the process. Oxford University's Research laboratory for Archaeology was similarly discouraging about the prospects of getting any meaningful results from their Particle Accelerator.

It was not possible to test and examine the bones themselves. However, Professor Wright's descriptions of the bones and an extensive photographic record made of them in 1933 offered a very sound basis for a re-assessment. David Bowen, Professor of Forensic Pathology at the Charing Cross Hospital Medical School in Hammersmith, West London, was approached to see if he would be prepared to undertake a re-appraisal of the available evidence. Professor Bowen showed great interest, but felt that such a re-appraisal was more properly in the territory of a specialist in anatomy and he suggested Dr Jean Ross, a Senior Lecturer in Anatomy also at the Charing Cross. Dr Ross willingly agreed to act as the medical expert. She was provided with a copy of the Tanner-Wright report and each of its accompanying photographs. She also received a copy of a report of an examination of the teeth of Anne Mowbray, Richard of York's child bride and a relative of both Princes, which was conducted by a dentist, Mr M.A. Rushton, in 1965. Anne

Mowbray had died in 1481, aged eight years and eleven months, and her tomb was undisturbed until 1964. It seemed possible that evidence about this authentic fifteenth-century child might throw some light on the two disputed skeletons.

A CRISIS

In January the prosecution witnesses, Dr Starkey, Dr Pollard, Dr Ross and Mr Richards, were each asked to prepare a statement and send it to the prosecution barrister. In accordance with the rules of English law, these statements were passed on to the defence barrister and his witnesses so that the defence could know the case it was to answer. Defence papers were not passed to the prosecution. Once Mr Russell, the prosecution barrister, had read all the witnesses' statements, he then interviewed them at length in his chambers in the Middle Temple. Out of these meetings the QC began to carve his strategy. Mr Richards would present a summary of events of 1483 from the death of Edward IV to the autumn rebellion, emphasising Richard III's fear and hatred of the Woodville family. Dr Pollard's task was to outline the probable fate of the Princes and to attest to the reliability of the two contemporary chronicles upon which the prosecution was to base most of its case: *The Usurpation of Richard III* by Dominic Mancini and *The Croyland Chronicle* Dr Pollard was also to tackle the knotty question of the pre-contract, to demonstrate that it was merely a pretext for the usurpation and show that the Princes still posed a threat to Richard's hold on the throne. Dr Starkey would have to wrap up the question of the pre-contract and to present and defend the version of events delineated by the Tudor historians.

In the beginning of February, barely three weeks before the trial, there was a surge of anxiety about the defence case. The prosecution barrister had been able to devote a large amount of time, working with the production team, preparing his case. The defence barrister, on the other hand, had had a series of demanding cases in distant parts of the country which precluded similar thrashing-out meetings. On the occasions when the barrister and his prospective witnesses had been brought together, the meetings were not successful. The heart of the problem was a confusion of roles between the barrister and the witnesses. The research team could provide any amount of background material to the QC, but he felt that the actual evidence of his case should come from the witnesses themselves. The witnesses, on the other hand, expected the barrister to select the areas he wanted them to deal with so they could prepare themselves accordingly. This state of affairs led to a crisis of confidence and action was needed to cure it. It was decided to hold an emergency meeting to induce a sense of purpose which it was hoped would boost the morale of the defence team and would convince the QC that he did have a viable case on his hands.

The crisis conference took place at the home of Jeremy Potter in Kensington. It was attended by Mark Redhead for LWT, Anne Sutton and Peter Hammond, the Research Officer of the Richard III Society. Jeremy Potter opened the deliberations with determined optimism by jokily remarking that the occasion would go down in legend as the Woodsford Square meeting when it was finally proved that Buckingham was the murderer of the Princes. One of the problems discussed was the division of responsibility among the various witnesses. Lady Wedgwood was to tackle the question of Richard's image over the years and, although it was thought this would be interesting and informative, and make a good sympathy-winning opening for the defence, it did not tackle the particular question of whether or not Richard had killed the Princes. Keith Dockray as a historian could offer some telling points on the bias and unreliability of information in the period generally but, having some doubts as to Richard's innocence, could not deal with the specific details of the disappearance of the Princes. The weight of the case was therefore resting upon the shoulders of Jeremy Potter and it was felt to be necessary to spread this load. In particular, Jeremy Potter was unhappy about tackling the technical issue of Edward IV's marriage pre-contract. But Anne Sutton was at home with first-hand research and had the experience and weight to be able to deal with the pre-contract. Though initially she had been reluctant to take part in the programme, she finally rallied to the cause. As well as taking on the defence of the pre-contract as a valid reason for Richard to take the throne, Anne Sutton also prepared a brief on Richard's benevolent achievements as King in his brief reign. It was decided to further strengthen the defence by officially asking Peter Hammond to join the back-up team to give us the benefit of his encyclopaedic knowledge of the subject.

A new-found resolve gripped the defence. Jeremy Potter, Anne Sutton and Peter Hammond went away to prepare critiques on the statements of all the prosecution witnesses as well as to come up with new ammunition on such questions as the death of Hastings and the behaviour of Elizabeth Woodville. Jeremy Potter also turned his attention to the reliability of the standard translations of Mancini and the *Croyland Chronicle*. The barrister decided to use a crucial point about the translations in his cross-examination of Dr Pollard.

The jury

THE JURY

As judgement day, February 21st, approached one major task still remained. The finding of a jury had been left deliberately until relatively late, as the story of such a strange enterprise might have been picked up by the newspapers and it was important to give the jury members as little time as possible to bone up on the subject of Richard III, so that they would come into the court with open minds. The trial required a crown court jury: twelve ordinary members of the public without any specialist interest in or knowledge of Medieval history. However, it was realised that they were going to be required to absorb a remarkable number of facts in a relatively short space of time and the barristers were not going to be able to spell out their cases as they could in a normal trial. A jury member totally bored by history might lose interest and fail to absorb any of the information. This probably happens as a matter of course in a real trial, but a sense of duty was felt to Richard III, his prosecutors and defenders, to give him a proper hearing. It was therefore decided that a reasonably intelligent layman's interest in history should be one of the qualifications for appearing on the jury. It was also considered necessary to try to minimise any geographical bias for and against Richard. As had emerged from the researches, Richard III was the only English King to have had a predominantly northern power base. It was feared that a wholly London-based jury might be unsympathetic to an alleged murderer from north of the Trent. Conversely, a northern jury might be over-sympathetic to a fellow northerner. It was therefore very important to achieve as wide a geographical spread as possible. It had been pointed out by many people, female as well as male, that Richard III had a particular appeal for women. Whether or not this is true, it was decided to obtain an even balance of men and women. It was also hoped to achieve a balance between young and old and between social classes. In short, to take that old cliché, 'a cross-section of Society'. In conjunction with London Weekend's market research department a questionnaire was devised which it was hoped would weed out those wholly unsuitable. A telephone research company took the questionnaire and made calls to all parts of the country until they had turned up around thirty potential jurors. The production team then called those on this short-list to make the final selection. Each person was questioned about historical figures mentioned in the questionnaire, to discover any views on Richard III without giving the game away. Those knowledgeable about the subject or convinced of Richard's guilt or innocence were discarded automatically.

Others were rejected on different grounds: a solicitor because he would not be allowed to sit on an ordinary jury and because he was likely to dominate the jury room with his professional skills and legalistic arguments; several teachers because no more than one was wanted on the jury. A travel agent was rejected because he was very well-informed about the Tudors and it was thought this might prejudice him against a Plantagenet. This operation, though time-consuming, provided an insight into the historical knowledge of the wider public. One respondent said that Richard III died after being thrown off a bridge, a confusion of the legend of his hitting his foot on a bridge on the way to Bosworth and his head banging the parapet on his return as a corpse. Another said that Richard's downfall was due to his 'very unfortunate choice of friends'.

The final twelve jurors were:

Men

1. An Indian-born hospital doctor from Bangor, North Wales. Aged 25–34.
2. An estate agent from South London. Aged 35–44.
3. A farmer from Bingham, Nottinghamshire. Aged 25–34.
4. A bookseller from Stroud, Gloucestershire. Aged 55–64.
5. A builder from Southwick, Sussex. Aged 35–44.
6. A company director from Sheffield. Aged 45–54.

Women

7. A student from Leicester. Aged 15–25.
8. A health survey administrator from Bristol. Aged 45–54.
9. A housewife from Southwell, Nottinghamshire. Aged 25–34.
10. A teacher from Chorley, Lancashire. Aged 45–54.
11. A clerk typist from Gloucester. Aged 45–54.
12. A housewife from Crewe in Lancashire. Aged 45–54.

Perhaps the mix could have been better; the 45–54 age range was over-represented, but on balance it was felt that a reasonably representative selection of people had been chosen to hear the trial.

Once the jury members had been selected they were still not told precisely why they were coming to London, though they knew they had to take part in a historical investigation of some sort. The penny dropped for some when they arrived at the hotel that had been selected for them in London, the Tower Hotel. One learnt the identity of the defendant from one of those founts of uncanny, though not necessarily reliable, information – a London taxi driver.

THE FINAL DAYS

His Royal Highness, The Duke of Gloucester, the patron of the Richard III Society, had agreed to introduce the programme and the Tower of London seemed the ideal place to record his words. The choice of locations in the Tower was limited. There were two options. One was at the foot of the wooden stairs that lead down from the Thames side of the White Tower to the open space below, where the Royal apartments once stood. It was beneath an earlier staircase on the same spot that the controversial bones were found in 1674. The second option was the interior of the Bloody Tower where, at least in the popular imagination, the Princes were kept. There may have been some truth in this story for, as the *Great Chronicle of London* reported, 'the children were seen shooting and playing in the garden' and the Bloody Tower was once called the Garden Tower. The director, Graham Williams, fearing that the English climate would certainly oblige with rain in February, chose the Bloody Tower.

After discussing what he might say with the production team, His Royal Highness wrote his own personal introduction to the trial, drawing attention to the fact that he is the first person since Richard III himself to bear the name and title of Richard, Duke of Gloucester. The introduction was recorded a few days before the trial and featured the Duke descending a spiral staircase in the Bloody Tower and speaking his words to the camera whilst standing next to the great portcullis which could seal the Tower from the rest of the world.

The final days before the trial were fraught: every available moment was filled with meetings between witnesses and barristers, visits to the set and last-minute panics over illustrations. Each witness was seen and taken through his evidence and, as the finishing touches were added to the arguments, the carpenters were adding the finishing touches to Old Bailey Court Number Four which they had built in London Weekend's Studio Number One. It was on a visit to the set on the evening before the trial that the defence QC revealed he had decided not to call Keith Dockray. Mr Dillon explained that, though Mr Dockray would have much of importance to contribute as far as an assessment of the chronicles was concerned, if the prosecution asked him the fundamental question: 'Do you believe that Richard III probably killed the Princes?', he could not be expected to lie. Keith Dockray took this news with his usual equanimity and cheerfulness. His considerable work for the defence was not wasted, for many of his observations on the chronicles and on the northern aspect of the case were included in the defence counsel's cross-examination.

This was the final line-up: The first witness for the prosecution was to be Jeffrey Richards who was to present a summary of the chain of events which drove Richard inevitably to the murder of the Princes. Dr Ross was to follow Mr Richards onto the witness stand with her assessment of the bones of 1674. Dr Pollard was to be called next to attest to the reliability of the *Croyland Chronicle* and Mancini, and to dismiss the pre-contract as a mere pretext for Richard's usurpation of the throne. The final witness to be called for the prosecution was Dr David Starkey who would deal with More and later historians.

For the defence, Lady Wedgwood was to appear first to show how Richard's image was distorted by Tudor propaganda. The defence barrister decided to call Anne Sutton next to defend the pre-contract as a legitimate reason for Richard to take the throne and to suggest the benevolence of Richard and his reign by reference to some of his legislation. Jeremy Potter was to appear last to attack the reliability of the chronicles, to suggest the villainy of Buckingham, to raise the question of why Henry Tudor failed to investigate the murder of his wife's younger brothers and to question the supposed confession of Sir James Tyrell.

On Tuesday 21st February, the day of the trial, there was an atmosphere of great excitement at London Weekend's South Bank Television Centre. Producers and technicans, who had seen literally hundreds of programmes put through the studio, caught the trial fever. Productivity must have been hit when, later in the afternoon, staff totally unconnected with the programme tuned into the recording on the television monitors in their offices and found themselves hooked by the court-room drama.

The participants themselves spent a nervous morning closeted away with their barristers for a final run-through of their evidence. As with teams before a cup final, pains were taken to ensure that the two sides did not meet until the trial itself. This, and the necessity of keeping the jury apart from the rest of the world, demanded a considerable feat of logistics and a small army of minders to steer everyone around LWT's maze-like building.

At two o'clock in the afternoon His Royal Highness, The Duke of Gloucester, arrived at our studios. He had planned to stay for the afternoon, but when the jury finally returned its verdict some eight hours later, His Royal Highness was still in the audience. The trial itself began at 2.30 p.m. and after seven and a half hours, with breaks for tea, dinner, for Lord Elwyn-Jones to prepare his summing-up and for the jury to reach its verdict, five and a half hours of videotape had been recorded. This was edited to a four-hour programme for transmission by Channel Four on Sunday 4th November, 1984.

The transcript of the trial that follows is complete.

HIS ROYAL HIGHNESS
THE DUKE OF GLOUCESTER'S
INTRODUCTION

His Royal Highness, The Duke of Gloucester

HIS ROYAL HIGHNESS
THE DUKE OF GLOUCESTER'S
INTRODUCTION

This is the site of England's greatest historical mystery. Five hundred years ago two young brothers, King Edward V and Richard Duke of York were brought here, to the Royal apartments, by their uncle to prepare for Edward's coronation. The boys were seen playing in the garden near to this building, the Bloody Tower or the Garden Tower as it was then called. Edward's coronation never took place, but their uncle, who bore the same name and title as myself, Richard Duke of Gloucester, was crowned instead. The young Princes disappeared from public view. According to the official history of the Tudors and of Shakespeare, they'd been murdered by their wicked grasping uncle. But historical research reveals that the story is much more complicated than this simple explanation. The hunch-backed monster that Shakespeare created provides wonderful drama, as history, it leaves a great deal to be desired.

1984 is not only the 500th anniversary of these events, it is also, because of George Orwell, the symbol of the state's potential for control of information to alter not only the present and future but also the past. Is this what the Tudors did to Richard III? Or was he truly a man so corrupted by the pursuit of power that he murdered the nephews he'd promised to support? This programme endeavours to examine this mystery, to penetrate the complications of the historical records and to examine the assumptions, the prejudices and the beliefs of certain eminent historians, by using the same techniques and methods practised by the best legal brains in our courts. They have the unenviable task of pursuing the possibilities and probabilities of events in a different age to our own; the witnesses dead and buried except for their written records, the motives of the authors open to question at every turn. What you are about to see is an attempt to examine objectively the evidence on both sides. Presided over by the distinguished former Lord Chancellor, Lord Elwyn-Jones, two eminent QCs will marshall historians and other experts to present the case for and against the King. A jury of twelve men and women will attempt to decide on the guilt or innocence of King Richard. It should be a fascinating experience. They do so with the knowledge that, whatever the outcome, the cells in the Tower will remain empty tonight. Five hundred years ago the outcome would have been rather different. Not only for the accused but maybe also for the witnesses and jury themselves.

THE
TRIAL

THE
TRIAL

CLERK OF THE COURT: The court will rise.

The charge is that King Richard III did, in or about the month of August 1483, in the Tower of London, murder Prince Edward,* Prince of Wales, and Prince Richard, Duke of York.

JUDGE: Mr Dillon, I understand that you represent King Richard III in these proceedings.

MR DILLON: My Lord, I do.

JUDGE: In view of his inescapable absence,† what is your plea on his behalf.

MR DILLON: My Lord, the plea is one of not guilty.

JUDGE: Members of the jury, in these proceedings you will be invited to deliver your verdict on a matter which has been the subject of fierce controversy and dispute for over five hundred years. It is whether or not King Richard III was responsible for the alleged murder, in the Tower of London, of the two young Princes, Prince Edward and Prince Richard. King Richard himself was killed on the battlefield of Bosworth in 1485; he is beyond the power and jurisdiction of this or indeed any other human court. What you are invited to do today, in these proceedings, is to pass a historical judgement upon him. He stands, in a sense, indicted at the bar of history. The charge against him as you've just heard, is one of the gravest charges in the calendar of crime: murder. We will as far as is practicable, follow the form of an ordinary criminal trial. However, as the potential witnesses to the events of the year 1483 are long dead, the strict rules of evidence

---

* Prince Edward strictly deserves the title of Edward V. After a debate that continued until minutes before the trial we decided to call him a Prince for the sake of clarity.

† The dock was empty. We could have used an effigy of Richard or an actor, but such devices would have detracted from the style of the programme: we wanted a present-day courtroom not a stage drama.

Mr Russell, the prosecution barrister

obviously cannot be complied with. And you may think in these circumstances there could never be any proof, to the extent of certainty, of the decision, which is always required in the ordinary trial before an accused man can be convicted on a charge of murder, or whatever it may be. You will therefore in due course be asked to decide this matter on the basis of probabilities, is it probable that King Richard murdered the Princes or not?* May I ask counsel whether that approach to the case is agreed by both?

MR DILLON: My Lord, it is.

JUDGE: Thank you very much. Then Mr Russell, do you open the case for the Crown?

MR RUSSELL: Yes, may it please your Lordship. Members of the jury, in this case I appear for the prosecution together with my learned friend Mr Godfrey, and as you appreciate, my learned friend Mr Dillon appears for the defendant, together with Mr Lott.† Members of the jury, in 1483, five hundred years ago last April, King Edward IV died leaving two young sons, the Princes, aged twelve and ten. The elder was proclaimed King Edward V, but he never lived to wear that crown. On his way to London to mount the throne, he was taken by his uncle, Richard of Gloucester, this defendant, and incarcerated in the Tower of London, later to be joined, under circumstances of which you will hear, by his younger brother Prince Richard. Within weeks the defendant had seized the throne for himself and the young boys, the rightful heirs, shortly afterwards disappeared, never to be seen again. Two hundred years later in 1674, their bones were found buried deep within the precincts of the Tower of London, and removed to Westminster Abbey, where they lie to this day. The prosecution allege that, whatever the manner of their deaths, who-ever actually caused them, they were murdered on the instructions of this defendant, innocent pawns in a power game which Richard had to win to survive. It is therefore alleged that he was a party to that foul deed, and accordingly is charged before you with the offence of murder. Now, members of the jury, before I commence the barest

* In view of the exceptional nature of our trial it was decided to drop the normal burden of proof used in English courts, guilt beyond reasonable doubt, because it would require a degree of certainty impossible five hundred years after the events. Instead we adopted the burden of proof required in civil cases on the balance of proba-bilities.

† For reasons of professional etiquette the two QCs and their assistants used assumed names for the trial.

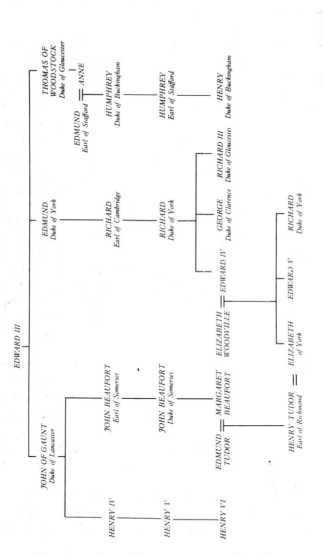

ITEM. Genealogical tree of the houses of Lancaster and York

outline to the evidence in this case, let me start by setting the historical scene, which I think is necessary. And hopefully you have in front of you a genealogical tree of the houses of Lancaster and York at this time. Your Lordship has it?

JUDGE: Yes, and it is in the blue folder.

MR RUSSELL: Members of the jury, fifteenth-century England was torn apart by the Wars of the Roses, a civil war between the rival houses of Lancaster and York, both houses descended from Edward III. And if you look at that tree, you will see Edward III at the top, and thereafter, under the first parallel line, two of his children: John of Gaunt, Duke of Lancaster, who headed the House of Lancaster, and Edmund of York, the House of York. And you will see that from the House of Lancaster came the three kings on the left hand side, Henry IV, Henry V, and Henry VI, Lancastrians. From the House of York, if you look down three generations, under Edmund Duke of York, in the centre, you'll find Richard Duke of York, and you will see that he had three children: Edward, to become Edward IV and succeed Henry VI, George Duke of Clarence, and Richard Duke of Gloucester, to become Richard III, this defendant. It was the defeat of Henry VI (far left hand side) by Edward IV, which established not only Edward IV, but the House of York from which he came, on the throne of England. Thereafter, for the next ten or eleven years, peace and prosperity reigned up to the year 1483. During that period of time, Richard of Gloucester, the younger brother of King Edward as you can see, was ruling the north.

Edward IV married Elizabeth Woodville, and again you can see just to the left of Edward IV's name the name of Elizabeth Woodville, an important character in this drama. He married her secretly, she had been married before,* and she was a commoner, and therefore it was an unpopular marriage. They had seven children, only three appear on this tree; she had a number of daughters, one in particular, Elizabeth of York, which you can see there, and also the two Princes, Edward and Richard.

The Queen's family, the Woodvilles, were ambitious and acquisitive, and Edward IV turned them into the most wealthy and powerful faction in the South and in Wales, thus in fact, although he may not

---

* Elizabeth Woodville was the widow of a Lancastrian, Sir John Grey, Lord Ferrers, who had been killed at the battle of St Albans. She had a large family including two sons from her previous marriage, five brothers and seven unmarried sisters all of whom required suitably wealthy husbands.

have known it, sowing the seeds of the violence and conflict which
was to come.

Finally there are two other characters, before we leave this tree, that
I must refer you to: far right hand side at the bottom, Henry, Duke of
Buckingham, an ally of Richard III, you see he was descended also
from one of Edward III's sons, Thomas of Woodstock. And equally
important, left hand side towards the bottom, Henry Tudor, to
become Henry VII, and to marry Elizabeth Woodville's daughter,
Elizabeth of York, descended from a Margaret Beaufort, again
through the line of Lancaster, John of Gaunt.

Well now, members of the jury, let us come to the death of Edward
IV. He died unexpectedly on the 9th of April 1483, his will nominating
this defendant protector to the new child king aged twelve, but
despite this it was immediately obvious that the Woodvilles were
determined to seize the reins of power through that boy. Lord
Hastings – I'm sorry to keep throwing these names at you, but Lord
Hastings, Edward IV's Chamberlain and Chief of the Guard (a very
powerful man in the establishment, but fiercely anti-Woodville,
although pro- Edward V) realised what the Woodvilles were up to,
and he called Richard from the north, as Edward IV had died very
suddenly. In the result Richard, together with his friend and ally
Buckingham, intercepted the king and his Woodville entourage at
Stony Stratford on their way to London. Earl Rivers and Sir Richard
Grey,* leaders of the Woodville faction who were accompanying the
boy, were arrested and the boy king was escorted by the defendant to
the royal apartments in the Tower of London, ostensibly at that time,
to await his coronation, but in fact never to emerge again.

The Woodvilles were now in disarray. Their two leaders had been
arrested at Stony Stratford, and Edward IV's widow, Elizabeth Woodville, fearing for the safety of herself and her family, took sanctuary in
Westminster Abbey with her other children, including young Prince
Richard. So Prince Edward was now in the Tower and Prince Richard
was with his mother in the sanctuary of Westminster Abbey.

The defendant then was proclaimed protector by the royal council
in accordance with the late King's wishes, and the date June 24th was

---

* Anthony Woodville, Earl Rivers, was the brother of Elizabeth Woodville, and
therefore uncle of the Princes. He was a scholar and patron as well as the leading
Woodville after the Queen. Sir Richard Grey was the second son of Elizabeth Woodville
and with his older brother Thomas, Marquis of Dorset, had been reputedly Edward IV's
companion in vice.

fixed for Edward V's coronation, Prince Edward's coronation. As I said, it was never to come about, because, members of the jury, there seems to be little doubt that by now the defendant had set his sights on the crown for himself. Hastings, who as I told you, although anti-Woodville, was loyal to Edward IV and his son Edward V, wouldn't countenance this. So what happened? What did Richard do? He had him arrested, and summarily executed without trial, an act which stunned and appalled not only the establishment in London, but also the populace generally. Rivers and Grey, the two Woodvilles who had been arrested, were also executed,* and the pattern was set, the Crown suggests,† the road to the crown by now already running in blood.

On 16th June, Elizabeth, Elizabeth Woodville, the ex-Queen, was prevailed upon to release young Prince Richard from the sanctuary of Westminster Abbey, on the pretext that his presence was required at his brother's coronation, but he was immediately, having been released, placed with his brother in the Tower, and the prosecution suggests, that that was all part of the defendant's scheme to get the young boys together in the Tower, so they would both be under his control. He'd now got rid of the Woodvilles, he'd got rid of Hastings, his main opponent to the crown, and now he had the King, Edward V, although not crowned, proclaimed, and his younger brother in his custody in the Tower of London.

What was the next stage, members of the jury? He then set about disinheriting the two princes, and you'll hear about this in evidence. I am going to deal with it now, again in barest outline. He did this by proclaiming them bastards, illegitimate children – upon the basis that before their father, Edward IV, had married their mother, Elizabeth Woodville, he had entered into a contract of marriage with another lady, one Eleanor Butler.‡ The evidence of this pre-contract, as it was known, was said to come from a Bishop Stillington and, if true, by the law of those days *that* could have nullified Edward's subsequent marriage to Elizabeth. I say 'if true', because the prosecution say it was a pretext – another one – but although it was not generally believed, it helped to clear the Princes away from Richard's path to the throne. And indeed, come July 6th, he was crowned king.

---

* Rivers, Grey, and others of the Woodville faction were executed in Pontefract.

† 'The Crown suggests'. This is an error of habit by the QC. The Crown was not of course involved in the prosecution of the case.

‡ Eleanor Butler was the widow of Ralph Butler, Lord Sudeley, and daughter of the Earl of Shrewsbury.

The usurpation had been ruthless, smooth, and efficient. But the Princes remained a worry, a thorn in Richard's side. Richard was considered a northerner, he had been up there, as I told you, for many years and he wasn't popular in the south. His position was by no means secure; there had been widespread concern at the way he had seized the throne. The Princes were therefore still a very dangerous rallying point for his opponents, and so, members of the jury, they were brutally murdered – probably in August of 1483, following the customary fate of all other deposed monarchs in the middle-ages, none of whom had been left alive by their successors.

Well now, why do the prosecution say the Princes were killed? Well members of the jury, to start with, they disappeared and were never seen again. And rumours that they were dead started in the autumn of that year and circulated widely thereafter, both at home and abroad. Did Richard ever produce them to scotch those rumours? No. Did he ever admit that they were dead? No. And why not, if they'd died naturally? Did he ever accuse anybody else of being responsible for their murder? No he did not. He remained silent, totally silent, a thunderous silence you may think, members of the jury, which in fact shouts his guilt.

But, members of the jury, proof of their deaths was established in 1674, when bones, almost certainly theirs, were found buried in the Tower. You will hear the evidence of this from a Doctor Ross, an anatomist, an expert, and again I will only deal with it therefore very shortly. In that year 1674, a chest containing bones was found by labourers ten feet below the ground, beneath or near a staircase between the king's apartments and the White Tower in the Tower of London. The reigning king at that time, Charles II, was convinced they were the bones of the Princes and had them placed in an urn, and placed in Westminster Abbey. In 1933, only fifty years ago, a leading anatomist, Professor Wright, was allowed to examine them and he found them to be the bones of two young children, aged twelve and ten approximately, who were blood-related, and you will hear the evidence of Doctor Ross about this; she has examined them from photographs only. You may think, members of the jury, that therefore, if that is right, the coincidence is too great for them not to be the Princes. And, members of the jury, you will want to ask yourselves will you not, if they were not secretly killed why were they secretly buried?

Members of the jury, before turning to the remainder of the evidence, I will just complete, if I may, the story of Richard's reign, because it is relevant; how he was overthrown by Henry Tudor – remember I pointed him out to you on the left hand side of the tree. He was overthrown by Henry Tudor in 1485. Henry Tudor had an obscure claim to the throne; if you just glance at that tree again, you will see it was through his mother, who was a Beaufort and descended from John of Gaunt. He had been living in Brittany during Edward IV's reign, and in October 1483 what happened was this: Richard's ally, Buckingham, changed camps, and led a revolt against Richard III, this defendant. Firstly the object of that revolt appears to have been to free the Princes from the Tower, and then, after rumours that they were dead, the cause of the rebellion changed to put Henry Tudor on the throne. It was a short-lived rebellion and totally failed, and as a result Buckingham was arrested and executed. Richard then reigned for another two years only. There was a second rising; this time it was actually joined by Henry Tudor and his supporters from Brittany,* and succeeded in defeating Richard at the famous battle of Bosworth. Henry Tudor then went on the throne as Henry VII, and married Elizabeth Woodville's daughter, joining the Houses of Lancaster and York, and ending that strife.

Members of the jury, the position therefore was this: those boys, we suggest, could not have been killed in the Tower without Richard's knowing, and if he knew, as he must, why did he not bring the culprit to trial, unless he was the culprit himself? Why did he not scotch the rumours and tell everybody what had happened to these boys, unless he feared the consequences for himself? He had already got rid of others in his way – Hastings, Grey – he had the motive also, the best and most powerful motive, that of the ultimate power in the country, the throne.

Now is this confirmed by contemporary or near contemporary records? This is the last matter that I intend to put before you at this stage. The two most reliable records known are the *Croyland Chronicle*, which we will be referring to in the evidence, and a record by an Italian called Mancini. The *Croyland Chronicle*, was written at a Benedictine Abbey in Lincolnshire and records the events of this immediate time which we have under consideration, without directly accusing Richard; no doubt because the writer, obviously a careful

---

* In fact Henry launched his second attempt on the throne from France. He had left Brittany in 1484 to escape arrest, which had been planned through a diplomatic agreement between Richard III and Landais, the Breton chief minister.

historian, had no positive proof. But he makes it apparent that his belief is that Richard was responsible, and he quotes from a poem that Richard destroyed his brother's progeny. Mancini – cleric, diplomat, historian – he was in London over the relevant months, from the death of Edward IV, until the day after the coronation when I think Mancini left to return abroad. He quotes the royal physician, a Doctor Argentine, that the young King believed that death was facing him (that's Edward V, Prince Edward), and that many men burst into tears when mention was made of him, because already there was a suspicion he had been done away with. But Mancini doesn't directly accuse Richard. He says, and I quote, 'But whether however he has been done away with, and by what manner of death, so far I have not at all discovered.' He had left London as I said, almost immediately after the coronation at the end of July, so he probably never had an opportunity to discover the actual details. But it makes it clear as I've said, as in Croyland, that he thought Richard was responsible.

One other record to which I must refer, and that is and probably the best known* of them – that of Thomas More in his *Life of Richard III*,* that was written after the event, about twenty years after the event, thirty years actually, I think it was. He gives a detailed and graphic account of the murders, and let me say at once, some parts of his account seem to be inaccurate, and therefore complete reliance cannot be placed upon the whole, and it has at times been heavily criticised. But it's an account you will hear from witnesses called by the prosecution, that should be taken very seriously. He, More, describes how Richard first sent a letter to Brackenbury, the keeper of the Tower, ordering him to bring about the deaths of the Princes, but when he refused, sent someone else, Sir James Tyrell, to do the deed. In the result Tyrell arranged for two servants, Forest and Dighton, to smother them, and they were buried at the stairfoot, 'metely deep in the ground under a great heap of stones', where in fact the bones were found, or near enough. And it is interesting to note that when Tyrell, who More was suggesting was actually responsible for killing them, when Tyrell was later executed by Henry VII, he was alleged to have confessed to causing the death of the two boys. Members of the jury, the accuracy of all the records about which you will hear can each in some degree be criticised, but we suggest that they all add up to a very formidable indictment, of this defendant.

* More's work is more precisely called *The History of King Richard III*.

Well now, members of the jury, that's all I intend to say in opening at this stage. The prosecution allege, and will prove: firstly the princes were killed in the Tower. That Richard had the motive, second. Thirdly, he had ruthlessly killed others on his way to the throne. Fourthly, they could not have been killed without his knowing, but he remained silent, and blamed no-one else. And finally, fifthly, contemporaneously he was believed to have been responsible as recorded by the chroniclers at the time.

Members of the jury, approach this matter with open minds. It's important that this defendant is tried fairly, and that he should suffer no prejudice from anything that you may have read, or seen, or heard in the past. Try this matter according to the evidence, which circumstantial and hearsay though it must be through course of time, we submit that it will drive you to only one conclusion on the balance of probability, and therefore, members of the jury, that evidence I will now call before you, so that you can in due course come to your proper verdict.

Mr Richards please.

JUDGE: Mr Dillon, in the circumstances of this case, you may think that the formality, indeed more than the formality, the procedure of taking the oath by witnesses, should be dispensed with. Do both counsel agree?

MR DILLON: My Lord, my learned friend and I have had the opportunity of discussing it; we both agree.

JUDGE: Much obliged.

MR RUSSELL: I think it unlikely the credit is going to be in issue.

JUDGE: I hope not . . .

MR RUSSELL: Opinions maybe, but not . . .

JUDGE: Not the bona-fides of the witnesses.

MR RUSSELL: Not the bona-fides.

JUDGE: Good.

MR RUSSELL: Yes, Mr Richards, your full name please.

MR RICHARDS: Jeffrey Michael Richards.

MR RUSSELL: And what are your qualifications?

MR RICHARDS: I'm senior lecturer in History at Lancaster University.

MR RUSSELL: Now, I want to ask you straight away about the events following Edward IV's death and Richard becoming king. First, in a sentence or two would you summarise your interpretation of those events.

Mr Jeffrey Richards

MR RICHARDS: I think the whole thing has to be seen in the context of the factional struggles which had split England in the late years of Edward IV and in the reign of Edward V. Richard moves to become protector in order to secure his position against his enemies, and when that proves to be insufficient, he moves to become king to further secure his position, and to maintain that position it's necessary for him to dispose of his principle threat, the Princes. And I think that one can see running throughout all his actions a continual thread, and that is fear and hatred of the Woodville clan.

MR RUSSELL: Well now you probably heard the way I opened this case, Mr Richards, and I was mentioning the Woodvilles. What was the power of the Woodvilles? How had they achieved this power?

MR RICHARDS: Through the marriage of Elizabeth to Edward IV, as a result of which he built them up with land, titles, position, until they had become a deeply entrenched factional interest. And by the time Edward IV died, and shortly thereafterwards, they were in direct control of the court, the council,* the Tower of London and the King's treasure, the fleet, and what is most important of all, the two Princes. And it was through the two Princes that they hoped to rule England.

MR RUSSELL: And I think I'm right in saying that the relatives of Elizabeth Woodville, the mother, had brought up Prince Edward and Prince Richard in the West country and Wales.

MR RICHARDS: Edward, Prince of Wales had been brought up at Ludlow by his uncle Antony Woodville, Earl Rivers, Ludlow being the administrative headquarters of the principality of Wales, and Richard Duke of York had been brought up by his mother Elizabeth Woodville at court. So to all intents and purposes these two boys are Woodvilles.

MR RUSSELL: Was there, was it clear at the time, I don't think we need go into this in any great detail because I doubt whether it's in dispute, but was Richard obviously concerned about the Woodvilles taking over in this way?

MR RICHARDS: He was, because . . .

MR RUSSELL: I think he made it clear; perhaps I could just lead you about this, I think he made it clear in a letter which he wrote to York, asking for men to come and assist him in London.

MR RICHARDS: Yes, I have that letter before me, if you'd like me to read it.

---

* The council was the formal grouping of the king's advisors, approximately equivalent to today's cabinet. It clearly acquires greater significance during an inter regnum, or in the event of a minor being on the throne.

MR RUSSELL: Well just read the relevant part would you?

MR DILLON: Is this a letter of 10th June that arrived in York on the 15th?

MR RICHARDS: It is.

MR DILLON: Yes, I thought so, thank you.

JUDGE: And written to the men of York, whoever they may be.

MR RICHARDS: To the citizens of York.

JUDGE: To the citizens of York, I see.

MR RUSSELL: Asking for them to come to London and giving as one of the reasons –

MR RICHARDS: 'To come to aid and assist us against the Queen, her blood adherents, and affinity who have intended and daily do intend to murder and utterly destroy us and our cousin the Duke of Buckingham, and old royal blood of this realm.'

MR RUSSELL: Yes, very well.

JUDGE: What was the date of that again?

MR RICHARDS: June 10th 1483.

JUDGE: Thank you.

MR RUSSELL: What had happened immediately after Edward IV's death in relation to Richard's protectorship of the new boy king?

MR RICHARDS: The council had met, the royal council, and dominated by the Woodvilles, had vested regency powers in the council itself, and had not appointed Richard as protector, and this clearly gave substance to his fears that he was going to be out-manoeuvred.

MR RUSSELL: Lord Hastings, who I was telling the jury was Lord Chamberlain and Captain of the Guard, was a very powerful man, correct?

MR RICHARDS: Lord Hastings was a pivotal figure at court, a pillar of Edward IV's court, and also of Edward V's.

MR RUSSELL: Pro-Edward, but anti-Woodville?

MR RICHARDS: Very strongly; he'd had two long and well publicised feuds with key members of the Woodville clan.

MR RUSSELL: Did he summon Richard to come south and assist?

MR RICHARDS: He urged him to come as soon as possible, to take possession of the king and assert his protectorship.

MR RUSSELL: And I don't think there can be any dispute about this; this was done at Stony Stratford, by Richard and Buckingham. Rivers and Grey, the Woodville escort, being arrested?

MR RICHARDS: Yes.

MR RUSSELL: How did Edward V (because he was proclaimed King by now, but perhaps we ought to call him Prince Edward still for convenience), how did Prince Edward react to that, the arrest of his uncle and half-brother was he?

MR RICHARDS: Yes, his half-brother. Gloucester and Buckingham explained why they'd done it, and they said the Woodvilles were plotting against Richard and trying to deprive him of the protectorship. And Edward replied that he found no fault in his relatives, and wanted to keep them with him.

MR RUSSELL: Yes. Now, I think the result of the arrest of the Woodvilles was that the Queen, Elizabeth Woodville, took the rest of her family into sanctuary in Westminster Abbey.

MR RICHARDS: That's right.

MR RUSSELL: Can you tell us in a sentence Mr Richards, what sanctuary was?

MR RICHARDS: All churches were able to give a measure of protection to fugitives from the law for a certain amount of time. Some religious establishments, notably Westminster Abbey, were able to give permanent protection to fugitives.

MR RUSSELL: So she should have been safe there?

MR RICHARDS: In theory.

MR RUSSELL: On May 10th I think the council then confirmed, after the Woodvilles had been disposed of, the council then confirmed Richard's protectorship.

MR RICHARDS: Unanimously.

MR RUSSELL: Coronation fixed for June 24th?

MR RICHARDS: Yes.

MR RUSSELL: Was Richard now secure?

MR RICHARDS: No, Richard wasn't secure, because the Woodvilles were still alive even if temporarily dispersed. Edward V had expressed his partiality for them, and Richard will not have been unaware of the fact that the two previous Dukes of Gloucester, both of whom had exercised power during the youth of their royal nephews, had both been disposed of once those nephews had come of age and taken power.* And Richard must have feared that if he carried on as protector and gave up when Edward V came of age, which he could do at 15, he might very well be for the high jump, because the Woodvilles would come back into power.

---

* The two previous Dukes of Gloucester were Thomas of Woodstock, probably put to death by Richard II, and Humphrey, murdered after his failure to retain control of the young Henry VI.

MR RUSSELL: Yes, so what did he do?

MR RICHARDS: Richard asked the council to condemn for treason and execute Rivers and Grey.

MR RUSSELL: Who had been arrested at Stony Stratford, and were being kept in custody somewhere?

MR RICHARDS: In Richard's castles in Yorkshire.

MR RUSSELL: Did the council agree to that course?

MR RICHARDS: The council not only didn't agree, but they expressed disquiet, that the King's chosen advisors should be kept under guard.

MR RUSSELL: And so what is your interpretation of what happened then?

MR RICHARDS: I think that this triggered Richard's desire to go for the throne; he couldn't be secure merely as protector, because the council wouldn't back his desire to get rid of his principal enemies.

MR RUSSELL: I think there is evidence from one of the Chroniclers, Mancini I think it is, that Buckingham then sounded out those in the establishment as to what view they would take of that course.

MR RICHARDS: Yes, Buckingham was the intermediary and he sounded first of all the most important, Lord Hastings, if he would accept Richard as king. And the answer clearly was that he would accept Richard as protector, but not as king.

MR RUSSELL: And what happened to Hastings in the result?

MR RICHARDS: Richard called a council meeting to the Tower, at which he arrested and summarily executed Hastings, and imprisoned those other leading members of the council whom he thought would have supported Edward V.

MR RUSSELL: What was the reaction to that?

MR RICHARDS: A shock of horror through the entire establishment, because this was an unprecedented act, to execute a major councillor in peace time, and not only that, the citizenry were also dismayed because of Hastings' popularity as a general benefactor.

MR RUSSELL: Keeping the matter chronological, on June 10th you've already told us, Richard wrote the letter to York, asking for troops, and I think they arrived shortly before the coronation.

MR RICHARDS: They did, the point was to threaten people with the arrival of this vast horde of northerners, and cowe London by the threat of their imminent arrival.

MR RUSSELL: On June 16th, Prince Richard – I won't use a word which might be indicating the suggestion to you – Prince Richard, was he *released* – let's use a neutral word – *released* from the sanctuary in the Abbey?

MR RICHARDS: Yes, he was. Richard now cowed the council, who were afraid of suffering the same fate as Hastings, and so they agreed to a delegation going to ask Elizabeth Woodville to release Prince Richard for the coronation of his brother.

MR RUSSELL: Was that a good reason or a pretext do you think?

MR RICHARDS: A total pretext as far as I'm concerned.

MR RUSSELL: Why?

MR RICHARDS: Because he wanted to get Richard Duke of York, who was the heir to the throne after Edward V, into his power, and into the Tower, before he could move to secure his own position as king.

MR RUSSELL: Well now, having got Richard from sanctuary, and into the Tower with his brother, and himself proclaimed king, was his position then secure?

MR RICHARDS: No, his position then still wasn't secure, even after he'd become king, because the Princes then represented a potent focus for rebellion and revolt. And this was the reason: that every other previous medieval monarch who had deposed a predecessor, liquidated that predecessor for fear that they would provide a focus for rebellion in the kingdom.

MR RUSSELL: That had happened had it?

MR RICHARDS: That had happened. Edward II was deposed by his wife Isabella, the she-wolf of France, and liquidated at Berkeley Castle. Henry IV disposed of Richard II under very similar circumstances when rebellion was brewing, and Henry VI had been done away with by order of Edward IV.

MR RUSSELL: And so the rebellion – that arose at what time thereafter?

MR RICHARDS: Richard's spies reported to him in the summer that rebellion was brewing. What had happened was that the accession of Richard III as king had changed the factional situation. When Edward IV died the Woodvilles and the anti-Woodvilles split over who should have power, but they both wanted Edward V as king. Now that Richard had become king and displaced Edward V, the Woodvilles and the anti-Woodvilles reunited with the aim of putting Edward V back on the throne.

MR RUSSELL: What was the reason for the rebellion initially?

MR RICHARDS: The reason for the rebellion was to free the Princes from the Tower.

MR RUSSELL: Then what happened?

MR RICHARDS: Richard's spies had reported to him (according to the Croyland Chronicler, who was a well placed government figure), that the rebellions were brewing to free the Princes from the Tower, and to free the Princesses from sanctuary. Now we know from the *Croyland Chronicle* that Richard took steps to make sure the Princesses couldn't get out of sanctuary, by ringing it with steel, and the logical corollary of that is that at that point he liquidated the Princes so that there could be no chance of them providing this focus for rebellion.

MR RUSSELL: Were there rumours at that time that the Princes were dead?

MR RICHARDS: Rumours spread shortly thereafter that the Princes were dead, but it was not known how. They didn't need to be known to be murdered, they needed simply to be known to be dead, so that there would not be any bid to free them from the Tower.

JUDGE: Where did the rumours circulate.

MR RICHARDS: I think if we can use Whitehall parlance, sources close to Richard III.

JUDGE: That's the old Fleet Street parlance.

MR RICHARDS: I beg your pardon.

JUDGE: Called 'usually reliable' I think.

MR RUSSELL: Did the revolt then turn to the support of Henry Tudor?

MR RICHARDS: Yes, the plan to scotch the revolt by allowing rumours to circulate that the Princes were dead, back-fired because the focus of the rebellion then shifted to an alliance between Elizabeth of York, the eldest daughter of Edward IV, and Henry Tudor, Earl of Richmond, the Lancastrian pretender. An alliance was brought about by negotiations involving Elizabeth Woodville.

MR RUSSELL: Let's just stop there a moment, and assimilate that if we can. What I think you're saying is that first of all there was the revolt to free the Princes, then there were rumours that they were dead, and in the result the revolt then was to support Henry Tudor.

MR RICHARDS: After he had married Elizabeth of York, yes.

MR RUSSELL: After he had married. And had there been an arrangement that that should happen?

MR RICHARDS: The arrangement was negotiated between Henry Tudor's mother* and Elizabeth Woodville in sanctuary.

MR RUSSELL: Now, Elizabeth Woodville in sanctuary had arranged for her daughter to marry Henry Tudor.

MR RICHARDS: And for them to take the throne together.

---

* Henry Tudor's mother was Margaret Beaufort, Countess of Richmond, widow of Edmund Tudor, Earl of Richmond. She was married to Thomas, Lord Stanley, who played a waiting game at Bosworth to make sure of joining the winning side.

MR RUSSELL: Would she have ever done that do you think, if she had not appreciated that her other two sons in line for the throne were dead?

MR RICHARDS: It is inconceivable in my view that she would have done so.

MR RUSSELL: Well now the position was that the rebellion was brought under control very quickly, and Buckingham defeated and executed, Buckingham having changed camps.

MR RICHARDS: Buckingham joined very late in the day when all this was well under way, but the rebellion collapsed quickly, and he was executed.

MR RUSSELL: Was Richard now secure?

MR RICHARDS: Richard was now secure, and this is demonstrated by the actions which followed this. In early 1484, he negotiated an agreement whereby Elizabeth Woodville came out of sanctuary with her daughters, and he also offered pardons to two of the principal Woodvilles, the Marquis of Dorset* and Sir Richard Grey who had been leading rebels, and whom previously he'd made every effort to capture. He was now willing to pardon them, the key fact being that the Woodvilles' key to power was possession of the Princes. And since the Princes had been put out of the way, the Woodvilles had no way of supplanting Richard.

MR RUSSELL: Well now lastly Mr Richards, you've told us how Richard had dealt with Hastings, Rivers and Grey; you've told us that no previous monarch in his position had ever behaved very differently. One final matter – Richard apparently remained totally silent when these rumours having started in the autumn of '83, continued thereafter.

MR RICHARDS: Oh, yes.

MR RUSSELL: Remained totally silent, how do you read that?

MR RICHARDS: It's very curious, because he made very strenuous efforts to deny rumours circulating that he intended to marrying Elizabeth of York,† and the fact that he didn't bother to deny these very abundant rumours both at home and abroad, seems to me to point to his guilt.

MR RUSSELL: If anybody else had done it without his condoning it, is there any way that he would not have been informed of that.

---

* Thomas Grey, Marquis of Dorset, Elizabeth Woodville's first son, had fled to France when Richard moved against his family on the death of Edward IV in 1483.

† According to Croyland, in March 1485 Richard was obliged by his northern supporters to deny that he intended to marry his niece, Elizabeth of York.

MR RICHARDS: Absolutely not, because the Lieutenant of the Tower, Sir Robert Brackenbury, was one of his most devoted followers.*

MR RUSSELL: And was there any reason, if he had known that somebody else might have done it for some other motive, was there any reason for him not to accuse that person?

MR RICHARDS: None.

MR RUSSELL: Yes, thank you Mr Richards.

MR DILLON: Mr Richards, part of your evidence is clearly based upon such sources as we have close to the time that we are having to consider, which is four months in the year 1483. Part of your evidence is based on your opinion drawn from the facts, however established, taken from those sources. It's notable I think, that you have referred to some of those sources, Mancini and Croyland in particular, about which I think the next witness is going to be giving evidence. But you have not at all referred to Sir Thomas More.

MR RICHARDS: No.

MR DILLON: Do I take it that that is, if I may express it broadly in this way, because you accept the opinion of Professor Ross, who is the Professor of Medieval History at Bristol University, I think. Can I quote the passage to you. 'More's highly elaborate account of the death of the Princes has long ago been dismissed as contradictory and deserving of nothing but scepticism.'

MR RICHARDS: I don't entirely share that view, no. I think that More is very interesting, but problematical. He's problematical in two ways: firstly because he is writing from the context of the court of Henry VIII, and secondly because he's writing in a literary style and form different from the *Chronicles*, which I have used. As a humble medieval historian I don't presume to trespass on the territory of Tudor court historians, and I think you may well be hearing evidence from one of our most distinguished court historians about how one places this in context. I don't think one should dismiss More out of hand, there are a number of interesting things in More, but I don't think I myself need to add More to the sources which I have adduced to convince myself that Richard was guilty.

---

* Sir Robert Brackenbury was a northerner who had been treasurer of Richard's household. Brackenbury became a member of Richard's inner circle on his becoming Protector. After Richard's coronation Brackenbury became Master and Worker of the King's Moneys, Keeper of the Exchange and Lieutenant of the Tower – richly rewarding positions previously held by Hastings. He died with Richard at Bosworth.

JUDGE: You don't dismiss him?

MR RICHARDS: No, I don't dismiss him out of hand, no.

MR DILLON: What would you say to this statement that 'More is full of provably false facts, and is too discredited to build on.'

MR RICHARDS: No, I don't think that is so, I think it depends on what you think More . . .

MR DILLON: Forgive me interrupting, Mr Richards, for time presses upon us. You do not accept that statement?

MR RICHARDS: No. Not entirely.

MR DILLON: I take it from the statement served which you have provided for my learned friend for the prosecution. They are your own very words that I have in typing before me.*

MR RICHARDS: Can you repeat them?

MR DILLON: Certainly with pleasure. 'It is' – meaning More's account written in about 1513, so 30 years after the event, and not intended for publication, we are led to believe – 'It is full of provably false facts, and is too discredited to build on.'

MR RICHARDS: Yes, well I wrote that in the early stage in my researches, and I haven't . . ., and since then I have re-read More, and I don't stand entirely by that, as I did. I think there are —

MR DILLON: I see.

MR RICHARDS: — difficulties and problems with More.

MR DILLON: Is one of the factors that one's got to bear in mind, when reading More, that he was brought up for a considerable period in the household of Morton, then Bishop of Ely, later to be made Archbishop of Canterbury by Henry VII?

MR RICHARDS: He was brought up in that household, yes.

MR DILLON: But, is that one of the factors that one has got to bear in mind, when one comes to read Sir Thomas More's account of the life of Richard III.

MR RICHARDS: I think it is, yes.

MR DILLON: Mancini said of Morton, that 'he was a man of great resource and daring, for he had been trained in party intrigue' – has a modern ring those words, has it not?

MR RICHARDS: It's the whole argument I've been putting forward.

MR DILLON: 'Since Henry VI,' but I am asking you about Mr Morton.

---

* As in any criminal trial the prosecution statements were supplied to the defence. Jeffrey Richard's first statement – a second was to follow – included the words quoted by Mr Dillon.

MR RICHARDS: Yes.

MR DILLON: Would you agree with that statement?

MR RICHARDS: He was an accomplished party intriguer, yes.

MR DILLON: Thank you very much. Now let me deal, if I may, very shortly and I daresay very inadequately, Mr Richards, with some of the facets that you have touched on and some that you have not yet mentioned at all.

Would you accept from me that by the 9th April, 1483, the date of Edward IV's death, Richard Duke of Gloucester, who I defend, then 31 years of age, had shown himself to be a good man. I use that layman's word deliberately. Good in relation to the common people, good in relation to his family, and his position of state.

MR RICHARDS: Ruthless in his carve up of estates to build up his power too.

MR DILLON: Anything else that you wish to add? I'm so sorry to interrupt. Anything else that you wish to add to that catalogue?

MR RICHARDS: As I say ruthless in his carving up of people's estates, including those of his mother-in-law, in order to benefit himself.*

MR DILLON: Well I don't know how one should act in relation to the estate of one's mother-in-law of course. Anything else you wish to add to that?

MR RICHARDS: I'd be disinclined to lock her up for life. Which is what he is alleged to have done.†

MR DILLON: That's precisely what Henry VII did with his mother-in-law, Elizabeth Woodville in due course isn't it.

MR RICHARDS: That's debated. She may well have retired to Bermondsey Abbey through ill health, it is said.‡ But again you'll have to consult Tudor historians I think on these matters, rather than, as I said, humble and increasingly discredited medieval historians.

---

* Richard's mother-in-law, was the widow of Warwick the Kingmaker (the Countess of Warwick). She was said to have been badly treated by Richard and his brothers Edward IV and Clarence. A law was passed in 1474 settling the Warwick lands on Clarence and Richard and declaring her to be, in effect, legally dead.

† John Rous, chaplain at Guys Cliffe accused Richard of locking the Countess of Warwick up for life in his *Historia Regum Angliae*, which was dedicated to Henry VII.

‡ In February 1487 Henry apparently stripped Elizabeth Woodville of all her possessions and shut her up in Bermondsey Abbey. One reason given was that she had betrayed Henry by surrendering her daughters to Richard, thus breaking her promise to him. Another theory is that she had plotted to aid Lambert Simnel, who had landed in Ireland in late 1486.

MR DILLON: I thought Richard had died before the end of the medieval period.

MR RICHARDS: The terminology of periods is a matter that is in dispute at this time.

MR DILLON: Let us not waste time upon that, Mr Richards, and let me turn then to another detail, for I shall call evidence upon Richard's status. He had, will you agree with me, at any rate this far shown himself totally loyal to his brother Edward IV? Therefore totally loyal to the Crown.

MR RICHARDS: Totally loyal to his brother Edward IV so far, but not loyal to the Crown under Edward V.

MR DILLON: Please, of course, add anything you wish in your answer. Let's go on from 9th April. The first thing that Richard did was to summon the lords and nobles of the north (for he was a northerner and was identified very much as a northerner by those in London and the south) to a requiem mass in York Minster requiring that those who attended immediately undertook an oath of fealty to the new king, Prince Edward.

MR RICHARDS: That's so.

MR DILLON: Came to London to undertake the post which had been imposed upon him by the will of his brother; namely as Protector to the infant Prince.

MR RICHARDS: Though that will have been set aside by the decision of council to vest the regency powers in itself.

MR DILLON: Yes, then that council then reversing that decision immediately after his arrival, on 10th May.

MR RICHARDS: And after the dispersal of the Woodvilles who had been the dominant factor on that council.

MR DILLON: Of course, of course, one has to bear all these factors in mind. He was advised by Hastings, was he not, to seize the Prince on his journey, for to secure the Prince would be to secure himself?

MR RICHARDS: That's right. Yes.

MR DILLON: It's right to give full weight to that fact, for it was the advice that Hastings gave him. A fact mentioned in Mancini, not alas, however, in Croyland.

MR RICHARDS: Hastings believed that that was what was necessary, yes.

MR DILLON: After his arrival he continued to act, having been appointed Protector, in the interests of the King to be, Edward V, requiring acts of fealty to be undertaken by those in London towards the King. And undertaking the first steps towards the coronation which one would expect. To begin with Edward was placed in the palace of the Bishop of London, close by St Pauls. The council resolved that he should be placed in the Tower, which is not the Tower as we understand it today. It was the premier royal household with many buildings around what we now see as the wall. It was traditional at that time that the king should travel to his coronation from the Tower.

MR RICHARDS: It was a royal palace at the time.

MR DILLON: Indeed. It was the premier royal palace of England was it not Mr Richards?

MR RICHARDS: I guess you could call it that, yes.

MR DILLON: It would be traditional of course that members of the king's family – the king to be's family – should travel with him from the Tower.

MR RICHARDS: Yes.

MR DILLON: Thank you.

Between then (we are now at the end of May), and the 13th June, comes that letter to which you have referred of 10th June, written to the Mayor of York in fact.

MR RICHARDS: Yes.

MR DILLON: Written by Richard, describing himself as the brother of kings and the uncle of kings, so that he was maintaining that same attitude of protector throughout. He was calling upon assistance from the mayor and the notables of York, for he had identified the Queen, her affinity and adherents as plotting against him and Buckingham. And if one reads the letter it is clear that he is asking for assistance for he fears not only the destruction of himself and Buckingham but also the interest that he represented, namely the north. That's correct is it not?

MR RICHARDS: Yes.

MR DILLON: Powerful support for Richard's fear has recently been uncovered. Only in 1980, in fact, in a fragment in the Royal College of Arms. Do you know the one to which I refer?

MR RICHARDS: No. You will have to refresh my memory.

MR DILLON: MS2 M6. May I read the relevant passage to you. There's a reference to Buckingham in it as well.

'In the mean time there was divers imagined the death of the Duke of Gloucester' – that's Richard the defendant – 'and hit was asspiyd.' I have to read the words as they existed; it means that it was found out does it not? 'And the Lord Hastings was taken in the Tower and beheaded forthwith.' The manner of his beheading can be criticised but within that there may truly be a reason for his beheading.

MR RICHARDS: As soon as the tumult started in London following the beheading, Richard sent out heralds to announce that there had been a plot, but there is no evidence of a plot, and you say 'the manner of the beheading' but there was no trial.

MR DILLON: I fully appreciate the latter but within that – and that fragment, as I stress again, only came to light in 1980 – one finds corroboration of Richard's genuine fear, does one not?

MR RICHARDS: The document to which you refer, as I now recall, is the commonplace book of a London merchant. He was recording the sort of views that were current in London. But the *Croyland Chronicle* which I believe is the work of, or is based on the work of Bishop Russell of Lincoln, who was a prominent figure in the government,* says that innocent blood was shed, and there was no trial, no judgement and that Hastings in effect was not guilty.

MR DILLON: Two views.

JUDGE: Is that the place from which this fragment came, namely the commonplace book of a London merchant? Is that what the origin was?

MR DILLON: My Lord, I believe not. But may I have it checked during the course of the court's adjournment?

MR RICHARDS: It is called the *Notes of a London Citizen* and it was found to be the commonplace book of a London merchant.†

JUDGE: It builds it up a bit more to say it came from the College of Arms perhaps, but we will find what the real origin of this is.

MR DILLON: He is certainly a London citizen.

MR RICHARDS: Not someone in touch with what was going on in Court.

MR DILLON: Yes. Two views to be balanced here, as in so many parts of this matter.

MR RICHARDS: I would be more inclined to give more weight to somebody who was at court and was a government minister rather than a citizen picking up gossip.

MR DILLON: So I understand you to say.

One last matter, can I just understand if I may, please. The time of the release of the daughters which is February and March 1984 – that's the daughters of Edward IV and Elizabeth Woodville, who were in

---

* Bishop Russell was appointed Chancellor in May 1483 and dismissed in 1485, shortly before Bosworth.

† *Historical Notes of a London Citizen 1483–1488* was found in The College of Arms by Professor Richard Firth Green, and published in 1981. The notes form part of a miscellaneous collection of papers dating from the sixteenth century and are probably copies of fifteenth-century originals.

Dr Jean Ross

sanctuary in Westminster Abbey – it was after Henry VII had attempted to join Buckingham in the uprising in October 1483, after it was rumoured that the Princes were dead and when the finger might have pointed at either Richard or possibly at Buckingham, or possibly at both, and after Henry VII had sworn on Christmas Day, I think in Rennes Cathedral, to strive for the throne of England and had undertaken to marry Elizabeth. Elizabeth was the eldest daughter of Edward IV.

MR RICHARDS: That's right.

MR DILLON: So it was in those circumstances that Elizabeth Woodville surrendered Elizabeth Tudor, or Elizabeth Woodville, her daughter, to the power of Richard of Gloucester, now Richard III.

MR RICHARDS: That's right. Because she was a canny political old bird and she knew she needed to survive.

JUDGE: I don't think you like Elizabeth Woodville very much do you?

MR RICHARDS: Not a lot.

MR RUSSELL: Thank you Mr Richards.

Dr Ross please.

MR RUSSELL: Dr Jean Ross, I think it's right that you're Senior Lecturer in Anatomy at the Charing Cross Hospital Medical School.

DR ROSS: That is correct.

MR RUSSELL: My Lord, before I ask this witness to tell us her conclusions in relation to the bones there is a matter of agreement which I think will save time and which my learned friend and I have discussed. It relates to the finding of the bones, and the statement, which I think Mr Dillon will accept, is this. That in 1674 two sets of bones were found by workmen in a chest buried under a staircase in the White Tower, in the Tower of London. I can let your Lordship have a copy of this if necessary. They were assumed to be those of the Princes and removed to Westminster Abbey. In 1933 they were disinterred for an examination by two experts, a Mr Tanner, the Keeper of the Muniments of the Abbey and Professor Wright who was then, this is 1933 of course, President of the Anatomical Society of Great Britain.

Dr Ross, I think it's right that you've had an opportunity of seeing and examining Professor Wright's report on his examination of the bones in 1933.

DR ROSS: I have.

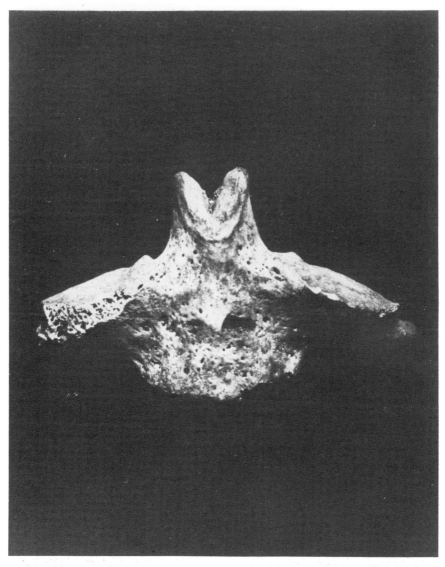

ITEM. The axis of the elder of the two children found in the Tower in 1674. It is 'lacking the tip because it is not yet fully ossified. . . . according to the appearance of his skeleton he was about the age of eight years, on this evidence'. Photograph courtesy of Dean and Chapter of Westminster

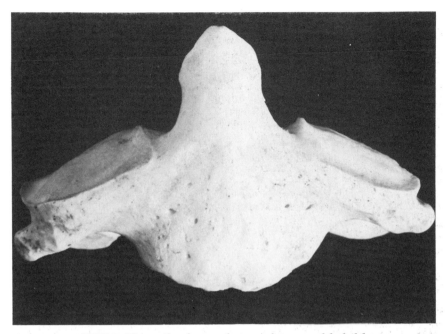

ITEM. The axis of a modern eight year old child

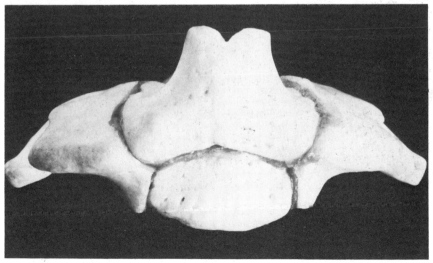

ITEM. The axis of a modern five year old child

MR RUSSELL: We are more concerned with your view in 1983/4. Therefore may we just summarize Professor Wright's conclusion in this way. I think based upon an examination of the bones, and particularly of the jaw bones and teeth or lack of teeth, he was satisfied they were the bones of two children, eldest twelve to thirteen, youngest nine to eleven.

DR ROSS: That's right.

MR RUSSELL: And I think he further concluded – although I don't think you are going to agree with this – he further concluded that staining on one of the skulls was that of blood and indicated suffocation.

DR ROSS: That is what he said.

MR RUSSELL: We are more interested in your view. You had an opportunity, I think, of not only seeing Professor Wright's report but also examining photos of the bones.

DR ROSS: Taken by Professor Wright.

MR RUSSELL: First of all, Dr Ross would you give us your two conclusions.

DR ROSS: I concluded that the ages of the bones at the time of death were consistent with twelve and ten years which were the approximate ages of the Princes and that there was some evidence that they were blood related.

MR RUSSELL: Now may we quite shortly – because I doubt if there will be a lot of dispute about this – may we quite shortly consider those two conclusions in relation to the age of the bones being those of twelve and ten. First of all I don't think you could tell what sex?

DR ROSS: No.

MR RUSSELL: And I don't think Professor Wright ever suggested either.

DR ROSS: No, impossible at that age.

MR RUSSELL: I think the two bones you particularly looked at was the axis. What part of the spine is the axis?

DR ROSS: It's the second vertebra of the vertebral column. The second one down from the top.

MR RUSSELL: And I think also the sacrum. Is that the big bit of bone at the bottom of the spine?

DR ROSS: That is so.

MR RUSSELL: Is 'sacrum' right or is it 'saycrum'?

DR ROSS: I say 'saycrum'.

MR RUSSELL: Well I'll say 'saycrum' too then.
    First of all the axis, I think you've got a photo of this have you.
    Now are those three photographs of an axis bone?

DR ROSS: They are.

MR RUSSELL: Is one – would you hold it up, it's probably easier just to look at it by looking at you – is that the axis bone of the elder of the two children.

DR ROSS: As judged by Professor Wright.

MR RUSSELL: And would you just hold up and tell us what the others are.

DR ROSS: This is the axis of a child of eight years old and you can see that the tip of the peg here is rounded and almost complete. Very different from this one of Edward which is lacking the tip because it is not yet fully ossified.

MR RUSSELL: So what you're saying is that it would appear from examination of Edward's axis that he was what sort of age?

DR ROSS: That according to the appearance of his skeleton he was about the age of eight years, on this evidence.

MR RUSSELL: Now the sacrum – would you look at that please?

DR ROSS: Yes. There was no photograph of the sacrum but Professor Wright said quite specifically that the sacrum which he believed to be that of Edward was incompletely developed. The first part of the sacrum has an arch at the back which is complete in an adult bone, but the sacrum that Professor Wright examined, the one that belonged to Edward, had the two sides of the arches fully half an inch apart which showed that the bone was not yet fully developed.

MR RUSSELL: And does that indicate the same sort of age as the axis did. eight or there about.

DR ROSS: Perhaps nine.

MR RUSSELL: So the bones would indicate two or three years younger than Edward's exact age.

DR ROSS: That is right.

MR RUSSELL: Is that unusual in bone development to have a two or three year difference depending upon a number of environmental factors such as health, diet and so on.

DR ROSS: Not unusual.

MR RUSSELL: Is it a better criterion to look at the teeth and jaw?

DR ROSS: It is indeed.

MR RUSSELL: Did you examine from photographs taken by Professor Wright and from his description, were you able to consider the elder and younger boys' teeth and jaws?

DR ROSS: Yes I was.

MR RUSSELL: What did you find in relation to the eldest boy's. In so far as age was concerned?

DR ROSS: The teeth showed that he was at least twelve years old and certainly not more than fourteen.

MR RUSSELL: Which would accord with Edward's recorded age?

DR ROSS: That's right.

MR RUSSELL: And the younger?

DR ROSS: He was at least nine and not more than ten.

MR RUSSELL: Again which would accord with Richard's reported age.

MR RUSSELL: Now in relation to blood relationship, your second conclusion. I think there was a missing tooth and upper pre-molar in Edward's jaw bone.

DR ROSS: On both sides.

MR RUSSELL: And a missing milk tooth in Richard's lower jaw bone. When we say missing, never there at all.

DR ROSS: Never there at all.

MR RUSSELL: Is that unusual?

DR ROSS: Very unusual for these particular teeth.

MR RUSSELL: And in addition what did that indicate to you.?

DR ROSS: A similar anomaly, if I may call it that, in the two boys would indicate that they were possibly blood relations.

MR RUSSELL: And I think there were missing teeth also in another young woman who died about that time aged eight and a half. In fact Richard's wife Anne Mowbray.*

DR ROSS: That is right.

MR RUSSELL: Was she a distant relation.

DR ROSS: Yes she was.

MR RUSSELL: She had missing teeth as well?

DR ROSS: She had very unusual missing teeth. Similar to those of Edward.

MR RUSSELL: So it would appear to be a family trait.

DR ROSS: That is right.

MR RUSSELL: And finally did you examine both the skulls. I think I need only ask you this. Did each of the skulls have a little extra island of bone at the back of both sides?†

---

* Lady Anne Mowbray was born in 1472, the daughter and heiress of John Mowbray, Fourth Duke of Norfolk. In 1478 she married Richard Duke of York, the younger of the two princes. She died in 1481, apparently of natural causes, aged eight years eleven months. In 1964 her body was discovered in a remarkable state of preservation. Before being reburied in 1965 a dentist, Mr M.A. Rushton, conducted an examination of her teeth, which was published in the British Dental Journal.

† The little islands of bone in the skull are called Wormian bones.

DR ROSS: That is right.

MR RUSSELL: Is that unusual?

DR ROSS: That is unusual too.

MR RUSSELL: Would that also indicate there was a blood relationship between the two children.

DR ROSS: Possibly.

MR RUSSELL: Well then can we just summarize your evidence in this way. Now I am asking you this question purely on anatomical grounds. Nothing to do with any other historical coincidences, such as we know the princes were there at the time and so on. On purely anatomical grounds what would your conclusion be?

DR ROSS: That the bones were consistent with being those of the Princes and that they very possibly were.

MR RUSSELL: But I think you would say that the anatomical evidence in itself is not wholly conclusive.

DR ROSS: Certainly the anatomical evidence is in itself not conclusive.

MR RUSSELL: The suffocation, the bloodstain on the skull, as found by Professor Wright; do you go along with that in any way?

DR ROSS: No, bones would not be stained by blood in that way and indeed Professor Wright himself tried to test the stains for blood and was not able to prove it.

MR RUSSELL: Thank you very much.

JUDGE: So we have no proof of the cause of death?

DR ROSS: None.

JUDGE: In respect of these young people.

MR DILLON: It's most unfortunate but in fact the President of the Society's conclusion – that's Mr Wright's – that there was a blood stain on the lower jaw simply cannot be supported.

DR ROSS: No it cannot.

MR DILLON: Secondly as you have made clear his further conclusion which would, if it was right, have corroborated Sir Thomas More's account of the death of the Princes, namely that they had been suffocated. His further conclusion that the presence of the bloodstain lends support to suffocation cannot alas again be accepted at all.

DR ROSS: Not at all.

MR DILLON: So that the view which has been current since his examination of the bones in 1933 on those two aspects alone has to be laid to one side now.

DR ROSS: I am afraid so.

MR DILLON: Completely. One can add to that of course, one would be in a very much better position if one was able today to re-examine the bones?

DR ROSS: Yes.

MR DILLON: And the teeth. For all the reasons that you have said?

DR ROSS: Yes.

MR DILLON: Are techniques developed today which did not exist in 1933, which would aid in this process of trying to establish their dates?

DR ROSS: Yes there are techniques.

MR DILLON: And the ages of the children?

DR ROSS: To an extent.

MR DILLON: We cannot, as things remain, date the remains at all. All one can say about it, doing the best one can, is that they are to be dated some time prior to 1674, which is the date that we are told they were found.

DR ROSS: That's right.

MR DILLON: Secondly the best thing that we can do is to say that they are the bodies of children because one cannot even sex them. One can't tell whether they are boys or girls?

DR ROSS: Not from the remains that are there, no.

MR DILLON: There is obviously a head-on contradiction between the dating which one gives, I am sorry, the ages one gives of the children at death, between the evidence from the axis and the evidence which one gets from the teeth.

DR ROSS: Yes.

MR DILLON: I know that you have seen Mr Wright's report. I don't know whether your attention has been drawn to the opinions of other experts consulted by Mr Kendall in 1955 and by Professor Ross in 1981. Have you been asked about their opinions?

DR ROSS: No, I don't know.

MR DILLON: Both have written substantial books on the period and both treat of the question as to whether the bones are the bones of the Princes. Can I just ask you about two things only. Mr Kendall in 1955 consulted an orthodontist – he's a specialist in dentistry – who said that the elder child was somewhere between eleven and thirteen; most probably eleven and a half according to the dentition, that's to say the teeth of course. But the terminology used by Professor Wright in his report is not altogether clear. Do you agree with that?

DR ROSS: It was clear to me in the sense that it described the development of the crowns of the teeth and the development of the roots of the teeth, and whether the roots of the teeth were fully developed or not fully developed. These are the criteria that are used for trying to tell the age of the bones.

MR DILLON: Well then let me ask you about Professor Bradford, who I understand to be a professor in dental surgery in Bristol, who expressed the opinion in examining the same material that you have (i.e., not the original material, only Professor Wright's report) that the elder child was not more than eleven if one assumes the child's average development. Now what we cannot do, alas, in the twentieth century is to know a great deal about the average development of a child in the fifteenth century.

DR ROSS: Well it happens that as far as the teeth are concerned there is some evidence as to the development of the dentition.

MR DILLON: If you please.

DR ROSS: From Anne Mowbray's skeleton. A very extensive examination was made of her teeth and it was established that they knew her age at death and the state of her dentition exactly corresponded with her age as we would have expected it to be today.

MR DILLON: But that applies to a female child and not the child under examination doesn't it? Must do.

DR ROSS: True.

MR DILLON: Well then I am just going to ask one final question. I understand it to be the opinion also of Professor Bradford that not much credence can be attached to the evidence of consanguinity. Would you like to comment on that remark of his.

DR ROSS: I don't know whether he knew of these anomalous teeth.

MR DILLON: Well he knew as much as Professor Wright knew.

DR ROSS: Ah. Professor Wright didn't know about the anomalous teeth because they were not described until 1965, I think.

MR DILLON: Thank you.

JUDGE: Is there any difference in the speed of development of the teeth of a female child as distinct from a male child.

DR ROSS: They are perhaps six months in advance of the males.

MR DILLON: And always remain so no doubt.

DR ROSS: Yes.

JUDGE: Thank you very much.

MR RUSSELL: Thank you Dr Ross.

Dr Pollard please.

Dr Tony Pollard

MR RUSSELL: Dr Pollard, I think you are the Principal Lecturer in History at Teesside Polytechnic.

DR POLLARD: I am only one of them. There are quite a few.

JUDGE: All principals?

DR POLLARD: No, lecturers.

MR RUSSELL: Dr Pollard, I want to come straight away to ask you about some of the contemporaneous chroniclers at the time of Richard's accession. Which of the chroniclers do you principally rely on?

DR POLLARD: Well undoubtedly Mancini and Croyland, the two most contemporary ones.

MR RUSSELL: Well then let me ask you about those. Mancini first. Was he an Italian cleric who was in London at the relevant time?

DR POLLARD: Yes that's so.

MR RUSSELL: I think he was there for about the first six or seven months of 1483?

DR POLLARD: Yes.

JUDGE: Briefly what was he doing in London?

DR POLLARD: Well he had probably come on an intelligence gathering mission. He was a close associate of Louis XI of France.

JUDGE: So he was well connected?

DR POLLARD: Yes he did have important connections in England.

MR RUSSELL: I think he subsequently wrote an account of those six months. The account of what he appreciated happened in London at that time.*

DR POLLARD: Yes.

MR RUSSELL: But that account was not discovered until fifty years ago, I think 1934.†

DR POLLARD: Yes that's true. It came to light in Lille at that time. The account was actually written before the end of 1483. It was written by the 1st December. And the important thing about it and the impact of its discovery fifty years ago is that of course up to that time everyone had been able to say 'Well the hostile views of Richard III came from people who were writing after the battle of Bosworth.' Here for the first time was a good coherent account written well before Bosworth.

* Dominic Mancini wrote his account for Angelo Cato, who was both a scholar and court physician to the Neapolitan King Ferrante and Louis XI. He was made Archbishop of Vienne in 1482.

† The document was found by C.A.J. Armstrong of Hertford College, Oxford, in the Bibliothèque Municipale in Lille in 1933.

MR RUSSELL: He was an Italian and did he have any grasp of the English language?

DR POLLARD: Not a lot we understand. He of course spoke Latin and, as I hope I'll show, he mixed with people who were his own countrymen who spoke English and also spoke, obviously, Italian to him.

JUDGE: Latin was the language of the courts and other places.

DR POLLARD: Well it was more not so much for the court as for government and er —

JUDGE: I said courts.

MR RUSSELL: He has been described by Mr Potter, the Chairman of the Richard III Society, as a man of integrity and an honest reporter. Do you agree with that?

DR POLLARD: Yes, a very sound judgement.

MR RUSSELL: What sort of sources do you think he had.

DR POLLARD: Well we know for a start that he had contacts in Edward IV's court. Also later on in the household of Edward V, in particular Dr Argentine, the King's physician,* a man, of course, who had inside information about what was happening around Edward V. This was a vital contact for him. He also, I think, would have been able to talk to fellow Italians in London, Genoese merchants we're pretty certain, and generally people in London.

MR RUSSELL: Well now, just one or two of the matters which he describes in his report; I think your Lordship has the relevant extracts and indeed my learned friend, I hope.

JUDGE: I have thank you.

MR RUSSELL: In relation to the Princes themselves does he record very early in the introduction to this record, does he indicate 'Richard Duke of Gloucester who shortly after destroyed Edward's children'.

DR POLLARD: Yes those are the words.

MR RUSSELL: Does he also refer in another place – this is the end of chapter five, my lord – to men bursting into tears? What's that reference?

DR POLLARD: Well he tells us that he observed people himself in the streets of London bursting into tears when they thought and contemplated the fate awaiting particularly Edward V.

---

* Dr John Argentine was a doctor and astrologer. He was the physician to both Edward IV and his son Edward V. Mancini refers to him by name. He later became Provost of King's College Cambridge.

MR RUSSELL: And he ends up with the words I think, 'Already there was suspicion that he had been done away with, whether however he has been done away with and by what manner of death so far I have not at all discovered'.

DR POLLARD: Yes that's a very good example of his honesty. He admitted that he hadn't been able to find out exactly what had happened though he suspected very strongly.

MR RUSSELL: And he left at the end of July, before the end of July 1483. Does he also refer to the – in the course of this story – to the death of Hastings?

DR POLLARD: Yes he does.

MR RUSSELL: Referring to the Protector 'rushing headlong into crime'.

DR POLLLARD: Yes.

MR RUSSELL: And I think there's a further quotation which starts 'thus fell Hastings'.

DR POLLARD: Yes and it's a very nice one, 'killed not by those enemies he had always feared but by a friend he had never doubted.'

MR RUSSELL: He clearly took a view about the death of Hastings.

DR POLLARD: Yes.

MR RUSSELL: Yes now, very well. Now turning to Croyland please. I think that was a chronicle written in 1486. Do we know who the writer was?

DR POLLARD: Probably Bishop John Russell of Lincoln.

MR RUSSELL: A very well connected person.

DR POLLARD: Yes, he had been, in fact, Chancellor for Richard III, that's the sort of chief minister of the Crown.

MR RUSSELL: But, whoever wrote it, does it come loud and clear that he was very high in government.

DR POLLARD: Very much so, a councillor. If it weren't Russell it was somebody else who had been in council.

MR RUSSELL: Does it appear to be very well informed?

DR POLLARD: Oh very much so, an insider's account. A man inside the government.

MR RUSSELL: Tending to give outline rather than detail.

DR POLLARD: Yes, it's a general memoir of a retired minister.

MR RUSSELL: Now I think it's correct that he does nowhere in that record directly accuse Richard.

DR POLLARD: No he does not.

MR RUSSELL: But does he quote from a poem?

DR POLLARD: Yes, there's a strange little poem right at the end of his account in which he states that 'Richard III destroyed his brother's progeny'.

MR RUSSELL: What interpretation do you put upon the fact that he included that particular poem in his record of these events?

DR POLLARD: That he was the cause of his nephew's ruin.

JUDGE: That he destroyed his brother's progeny goes a little farther than that?

DR POLLARD: Well I think many people would argue that.

MR RUSSELL: At that time – when I say at that time I think to be precise on January 15th, 1484 – did the French Chancellor in France make an observation in public?

DR POLLARD: Of a very similar kind. The States-General of France had met then. He said the children of King Edward were killed with impunity and the crown transferred to their murderer.*

MR RUSSELL: And Phillip Commynes – I think a French Historian, a writer of European History, at that time?†

DR POLLARD: Yes.

MR RUSSELL: Does he accuse both Richard and Buckingham of being a party to this matter?

DR POLLARD: He tells us that Richard barbarously murdered his nephews and he also says that the deed was actually done by the Duke of Buckingham on Richard's orders. The implication was *on his orders.*

MR RUSSELL: Well now the other matter about which I want to ask you is the question of the pre-contract. First of all, and if you can simply in just a sentence or two Dr Pollard, tell us what was the position of a pre-contract of marriage in canon law.

DR POLLARD: Well I think it's been well established fairly recently that there are two basic kinds of pre-contract that we are talking about. One is simply when a man and woman become man and wife by a simple exchange of vows and statements saying 'I do marry you'. In effect what takes place in the church service today. The other, and the one which I suspect is relevant in this case, is where a promise to marry is made. And it is significant in this respect that once a promise

* This was a speech given to the States-General of France by the Chancellor, Guillaume de Rochefort, at Tours.

† *The Memoires* of Philippe de Commynes cover European history between 1464 and 1498. Like Mancini's account, his history was intended for Angelo Cato, who planned to write a life of Louis XI. A politician and diplomat, Commynes moved in the highest circles, first in Burgundy and later in France.

is made, if the couple then nip into bed, then I think it is said that the marriage is a genuine one. So sexual intercourse has to follow the promise.

MR RUSSELL: Yes, so then it becomes a valid contract.

DR POLLARD: Then it becomes a valid contract.

MR RUSSELL: What were the facts here again if you could outline them very shortly to us?

DR POLLARD: Well I think we here must refer to the *Titulus Regius*.* Now that's the formal act of parliament which laid down Richard's claim to the throne, where he put down strictly for the record what the situation was, as he wished to say it was. And in this document he says Edward IV was pre-contracted to Eleanor Butler. That therefore the marriage to Elizabeth Woodville was invalid. Therefore the sons of that marriage, the Princes, were bastards. Therefore they could not inherit the throne. And thus he, Richard, held the title because his elder brother, Duke of Clarence had been attainted and therefore there was no-one else between him and the throne.

MR RUSSELL: When you say his elder brother had been attainted, Clarence I think had been accused of treason and therefore, in that way, had been disinherited.† So after Edward IV, Richard was the proper king.

DR POLLARD: Yes.

MR RUSSELL: Yes and I think we get that version about this pre-contract also in Mancini and Croyland.

DR POLLARD: We get a version of it in Mancini, yes.

MR RUSSELL: Now what I really want to ask you is this. This suddenly arose in the middle of June of 1483. Had anybody ever made this suggestion before?

DR POLLARD: No.

MR RUSSELL: That there had been a pre-contract and therefore that Edward IV and Elizabeth Woodville's marriage was invalid?

* Richard formally set out his title to the throne in an Act of Settlement, the *Titulus Regius*, which was passed by Richard's only parliament on January 23, 1484.

† Attainder for treason in the fifteenth century almost invariably meant death and the forfeiture of all possessions. Descendants of the attainted also lost rights of inheritance to land and titles. Attainders were reversible, but restitution in full was not easy to achieve. George, Duke of Clarence was attainted for treason in 1478 by his brother Edward IV. He was executed in private in the Tower of London, according to Shakespeare by drowning in a butt of malmsey. His 'bones' lie in Tewkesbury Abbey, and researchers from the University of Warwick have been attempting to establish their authenticity.

DR POLLARD: Not this specifically.

MR RUSSELL: Do we know where the source of this suggestion came from in June 1483?

DR POLLARD: Well we know from Commynes that it was Bishop Robert Stillington.

MR RUSSELL: That's Phillip de Commynes who you mentioned before?

DR POLLARD: The man we've just mentioned, yes, who was Bishop of Bath and Wells. And in fact that's confirmed by record sources of 1485.*

MR RUSSELL: That Bishop Stillington was the source of this information having been a witness to the pre-contract.

DR POLLARD: That is right, he says he was the only witness.

MR RUSSELL: So that was one thing which was being suggested. At any stage prior to Richard taking the throne did he attempt to bastardize the Princes in any other way.

DR POLLARD: Well there's a certain problem here of getting back five hundred years and understanding what went on. But Mancini has a very interesting version of the events. He says that first of all certain priests, who he describes as 'corrupt', stated that Edward was conceived in adultery and was in every way unlike his father, and Richard on the other hand was altogether resembling his father.

MR RUSSELL: Let's just follow that. There were two matters raised here. First that the Princes were bastards because of the pre-contract of their father before he married their mother, Elizabeth Woodville, and secondly that Edward IV himself was a bastard because he had been conceived in adultery.

DR POLLARD: Yes.

MR RUSSELL: Was that pursued, that second one?

DR POLLARD: No the second one was dropped. There are some indications that the mother was a little upset at the suggestion.

MR RUSSELL: I can believe that.

DR POLLARD: And there's some indication that they decided to drop the story quickly, it was too hot.

MR RUSSELL: And there was no reference to it in the *Titulus Regius*.

DR POLLARD: Not really, no. But they still slip in that Richard was the undoubted son.

---

* According to a report in the *Hilary Term Year Book, Henry VII Appendix No 75*, Justices in the Exchequer and the Lords in Parliament met to discuss Richard's *Titulus Regius*. They concluded that 'the Bishop of Bath made the Bill'. This was noted by S.B. Chrimes in *English Constitutional Ideas in the 15th Century*, (Cambridge 1936).

MR RUSSELL: Well now I think what happened was that on 22nd June – the two Princes having been placed together in the Tower on 16th June, I think I'm right in saying, and the coronation of Richard being three weeks later on the 6th July – on 22nd June was it not, that a priest, Dr Shaw, preached at St Paul's Cross the bastardy of these princes.

DR POLLARD: Yes, it's possible of course that that's the sermon that Mancini knew about which raised the other issue.

MR RUSSELL: And refers to as 'corrupt'.

I think on the 24th June, Buckingham was talking to the city, the city gentlemen at the Guildhall, in the same tones.

DR POLLARD: Yes that's when the story changes.

MR RUSSELL: And Buckingham two days later again to an assembly of the Lords.

DR POLLARD: Yes.

MR RUSSELL: Who had no doubt assembled or were assembling for the coronation.

DR POLLARD: Yes.

MR RUSSELL: And was that accepted?

DR POLLARD: Yes people did accept it.

MR RUSSELL: I would just like to refer to what Mancini said about that, if I can find my reference to it – if you'll just forgive me one moment.

JUDGE: You say that the assembly accepted the position, that the two young Princes were bastards.

DR POLLARD: Yes, there was going to be a parliament you see, planned immediately after the supposed coronation of Edward V, that's the normal thing. And many people had come to London, up to London, for both the coronation and the parliament, so in fact there were gathered in London some peers of the House of Lords, and many people who had been elected as members of the parliament, which of course never met.

JUDGE: It's a gathering of people of importance who had sprung up so to speak.

DR POLLARD: Yes, that's right.

MR RUSSELL: But, do we find that Mancini says that 'these matters having been raised, that he sought the crown for himself, on hearing this the Lords consulted their own safety, warned by the example of Hastings, perceiving the alliance of the two Dukes, Richard and Buckingham, Gloucester and Buckingham. Whose power supported by a multitude of troops would be difficult and hazardous to resist.'

DR POLLARD: Yes. I think it could be said that the Duke of Buckingham and Richard made them an offer they couldn't refuse.

MR RUSSELL: So finally, Dr Pollard, I think the position was this – you say, there was upon the basis, that the pre-contract was genuine or pretext —

DR POLLARD: A pretext.

MR RUSSELL: — confusion as to the story?

DR POLLARD: That's right, absolutely.

MR RUSSELL: What should have happened legally?

DR POLLARD: Well the facts of the case, concerning matrimonial law, should have gone to an ecclesiastical court.

MR RUSSELL: To establish whether these facts were correct or not, about the pre-contract.

DR POLLARD: That's right, yes, but that having been done, it was then normal for a lay court such as parliament, to rule on questions of inheritance.

MR RUSSELL: But that didn't happen in this case.

DR POLLARD: Neither, well the first didn't happen.

MR RUSSELL: Did Stillington ever give evidence anywhere?

DR POLLARD: There was no record that he was ever examined by anybody.

MR RUSSELL: And as we have seen, Mancini was explaining upon what basis the Lords of London accepted it.

DR POLLARD: Yes.

MR RUSSELL: And did Mancini and Croyland, from the two quotes you've already given us, did they appear to believe it or not?

DR POLLARD: Well neither of them did, and I think we've seen the way Mancini didn't, the Croyland Chronicler quite bluntly calls it, 'the colour for this act of usurpation'. He tells us he believes it was a bill invented in the north, and he goes on to suggest that the Duke of Gloucester was the sole mover, of what he describes as 'these seditious and disgraceful proceedings.'

MR RUSSELL: And lastly this; upon the basis of whether it was genuine or a pretext. Even if it was technically an invalid marriage, because of a pre-contract . . .

DR POLLARD: Yes.

MR RUSSELL: Could parliament at any time have reversed it, and thereby legitimise the children again?

DR POLLARD: Yes, it could have done, and of course it was to do so subsequently under Henry VII.

MR RUSSELL: So as soon as Henry VII deposed Richard at Bosworth, he reversed the bastardy.

DR POLLARD: Yes.

MR RUSSELL: Thank you.

MR DILLON: If it please your Lordship, let me deal with the pre-contract first of all if I may please. The position about Edward IV's mother was this, in one part of the chronicle of Mancini, the Italian spy reporting to the French court through his employer, a gentleman called Cato, who was Bishop of . . . can you remind me?

DR POLLARD: Vienne.

MR DILLON: Vienne, thank you, in France. At an earlier part in his chronicle, he reports the fury of Edward IV's mother, upon hearing of Edward IV's clandestine marriage to Eleanor Butler,* roundly declaring that Edward IV was a bastard, and that she was prepared to give evidence to support that statement.

DR POLLARD: That's an interesting point. That's something that is supposed to have been said by the very pious Cecily, Duchess of York, twenty years earlier. It is to be doubted really whether the story has any truth to it. Mancini himself twenty years after the event —

MR DILLON: It may be so, but that is one of the events that we have to bear in mind. It had some credence, because it was supported, was it not, by Charles of Burgundy, as far back as 1475. Mancini reports earlier in his chronicle, quite a separate part of the chronicle, that Cecily, that is the mother of Edward IV and of Clarence and Richard of course, had been so incensed by Edward's clandestine secret marriage to Eleanor Butler that she had loudly declared that he was a bastard, and that she was prepared to give evidence to that effect didn't she?

DR POLLARD: That was a story which Mancini repeats twenty years after the event, and I think can't be trusted, because it's so long after the supposed saying of those words.

MR DILLON: Well, without doubt it was a fact known to, possibly believed by, some people at that time.

DR POLLARD: Not a fact, a slurr. What is important about this, is that it was frequently, rumour was frequently put around by the enemies of the

---

* In the story which Mancini quotes, Cecily was not enraged at the secret marriage between Edward and Eleanor Butler, but between Edward and Elizabeth Woodville. The barrister appears to have confused the disputed Eleanor Butler marriage with the genuine Woodville marriage.

King that he was not true king, that he was a bastard or something like this. These stories had been around in the 1460s, and in the early 1470s.

MR DILLON: Then let me come on to the question of the pre-contract itself if I may please. There is no doubt that if in fact there had been a pre-contract, it presented valid grounds for invalidating the marriage between Edward and Elizabeth Woodville . . .

DR POLLARD: If, yes.

MR DILLON: And it would provide valid grounds for passing over the Princes' succession.

DR POLLARD: Not necessarily.

MR DILLON: If it could be established.

DR POLLARD: It would have been quite possible in fact, for parliament, to have simply declared –

MR DILLON: That I appreciate.

DR POLLARD: – that he was a true king.

MR DILLON: Parliament could in fact decide, although the levels of their, or the areas of their competence were not exactly defined by that time in the medieval period that we are dealing with. Subsequently it did in fact rule upon royal matrimony, did it not.

DR POLLARD: It ruled on certain issues of royal matrimony after the break with Rome.

MR DILLON: Edward IV was a man who was a known philanderer, to use a polite term. Croyland reported him as indulging his passions and his desires too intemperately. Even Mancini said, with his access to inside information, that he was licentious in the extreme.

DR POLLARD: Yes, he was.

MR DILLON: So it was a claim which could be believed of Edward?

DR POLLARD: Not really, I think a licentious man like that is likely to get his way without having to make up, you know, to go through the business of a pre-contract.

MR DILLON: This was a lady, the story went, who was resisting his blandishments, who would not succumb to him. It was said, so keen was he to procure her that he even broke off a hunting trip, which he, Edward V, would not ordinarily do.*

JUDGE: That would have been the ultimate sacrifice.

MR DILLON: Well, wild beasts escaped on this occasion.

DR POLLARD: Several stories like that were told about Edward V in fact.

---

* The lady who reportedly tempted Edward away from the chase, was not Lady Eleanor Butler but his wife to be, Elizabeth Woodville.

MR DILLON: He did not attempt after the death of Eleanor Butler, who died in a nunnery in, I think, Norwich –

DR POLLARD: I'm not sure where she died.

MR DILLON: – In 1468 –

DR POLLARD: That's right.

MR DILLON: – to marry the Queen Elizabeth Woodville, in public.

DR POLLARD: No, I don't think it's quite understandable that, after all, what we are supposed to understand is this is a highly secret, the whole . . .

MR DILLON: Precisely so.

DR POLLARD: Only Eleanor Butler and this Robert Stillington are supposed to have known. Now I'm not sure about you Mr Dillon, but I would probably, having gone through something like this with another lady, have preferred to keep it quiet, and not troubled my wife with the details.

MR DILLON: Exactly so. If he was to broadcast it, he would have been sowing seeds of discontent, there would have been a section of the public who would never have accepted whatever was said to have been the position. It would have been opening a can of worms.

DR POLLARD: But the thing in fact was a tissue of lies.

MR DILLON: Let's understand . . .

DR POLLARD: It's a tissue of lies.

MR DILLON: Let's understand if you please, because thereafter Henry VII took great pains to suppress the story after 1485. Can I examine the evidence with you briefly?

DR POLLARD: What happened in 1485?

MR DILLON: Yes.

DR POLLARD: Yes.

MR DILLON: Because it implied . . .

JUDGE: You say the pre-contract story is a tissue of lies.

DR POLLARD: Oh yes, everyone believed it at the time. I mean everyone knew it was a tissue of lies, they didn't believe the story.

JUDGE: Not apparently the Bishop of Stillington.

DR POLLARD: No, this 'bad wicked Bishop' as Commynes called him.

JUDGE: Oh dear, we are getting into deep water.

MR DILLON: I respectfully suggest that he is not a bad or a wicked bishop at all and that it is necessary for one, if one is going to take a fair and balanced view, to examine the evidence which is available. I have not much time. May I try and examine some of it very quickly.

DR POLLARD: Please.

MR DILLON: In the *Titulus Regius*, which you have pointed out to the jury was the act of parliament confirming Richard's coronation, which referred to the illegitimacy and the reason for the illegitimacy. Upon Henry VII's accession, he ordered that all copies be destroyed, under pain of heavy punishment, so that, and I quote, 'As all things said and remembered in the said bill and act, therefore, maybe for ever out of remembrance and also forgot.'

DR POLLARD: It was such a gross slander against his queen.

MR DILLON: I am not criticising.

DR POLLARD: Or libel I should say, should I not.

MR DILLON: I am examining it, with the jury, with your assistance. At the same time, the justices of the exchequer division, that is to say judges of the country, appointed by the King, together with the Lords in parliament, considered the *Titulus Regius*, considered the pre-contract, and came to the conclusion that the Bishop of Bath, that is Bishop Stillington, made the Bill. In other words he was responsible for providing the information which gave the grounds for the Bill, which gave valid grounds, if they existed, for Richard to ascend the throne. The Lords intended to summon Stillington before them, so that they could examine him. That would have provided a valid occasion, a proper occasion upon which Stillington's claim in relation to the pre-contract could have been explored, whether satisfactorily or not – and from which one could have possibly learned whether the pre-contract story was in fact the truth. Didn't it?

DR POLLARD: It's a very neat statement. The only problem, as I see it, is why, oh why was this not done in June 1483, when it really mattered.

MR DILLON: Because I'm asking about Henry VII, you'll understand. The examination did not take place because Henry VII refused, saying that he, the King, had pardoned Bishop Stillington and yet – will you follow me – one of the first warrants issued after Bosworth and the victory there of Henry VII, was to arrest the Bishop, and the Bishop was in fact arrested in York, within five days of the battle of Bosworth. It means does it not – let me put this as low as I can – that in one view, Henry VII himself prevented, or at any rate avoided, investigation into the claim about the pre-contract, does it not.

DR POLLARD: Carry on.

MR DILLON: That's the question.

DR POLLARD: Ah, well, what I think we have got to bear in mind about this, is that Henry . . . You have thrown in so many different things, it's very difficult to know where to start.

MR DILLON: I have stated to you a number of facts.

DR POLLARD: Interpretations of the past if I may say so. But in fact I think we have got to bear in mind that Henry, in 1485, was endeavouring to start his reign on a fresh start, a clean slate. He wished to, as his early statements made absolutely clear, he wished to get all the old quarrels and disputes between his subjects forgotten and put behind. And I think this is a piece with this policy, to start straight away by saying right we won't go over all this stuff again. The fact is that no-one believed it. He had passed an act of parliament which quite simply reversed it without discussing it in detail, married Elizabeth of York, who became his Queen and then continued to start afresh. There was no need in fact.

MR DILLON: Well I must go on to other matters, anxious though I would be to comment upon your answers. Let me turn to the Chancellor of France. The statement that you have taken comes from a statement made by him, Guillaume de Rochefort, in January 1484.

DR POLLARD: True.

MR DILLON: In which it was said that the children, Edward and Richard had been murdered, and 'their assassin crowned by the people's will'. Even in 1484 alas, there was no love lost between the French and the English. This was an extract from a long speech made by Guillaume in which he was holding up this example of democracy, yes, I respectfully suggest, to the French, warning them perhaps of the perils yet to come of the French Revolution if the lords and the nobles in France gave way to the will of the people. That's what he was warning them about. That's all the importance that can be attributed, I respectfully suggest, to that source.

DR POLLARD: There is another particular angle to it, I think, which one has to bear in mind and that is that the nature of the French monarchy in the 15th century which was almost sacrosanct, in which no king had been deposed since the eighth or ninth century. And what they were concerned about in 1484, when there was a minor on the throne, just as Edward V had been, was to make sure that the nobles and others in France would not imitate Richard of Gloucester in 1483 in England and wished to emphasise that in France we do things differently. In France we respect our monarchy and people inherit according to their due right, not as in the case of England where kings get deposed pretty regularly.

MR DILLON: I must pass on. Can I ask the most simple question about it?

DR POLLARD: Yes.

MR DILLON: Is the view not possible that what he was delivering to his audience was an example message. Is that view not possible in your view?

DR POLLARD: Yes but it leaves . . .

MR DILLON: Thank you. Can I pass to Croyland please.

JUDGE: It was an immensely political occasion anyway wasn't it in France?

DR POLLARD: Yes indeed.

MR DILLON: Can I pass to Croyland if you please. Neither Mancini nor Croyland identify Richard as being responsible for the death of the Princes.

DR POLLARD: This is true. Neither say directly he killed them.

MR DILLON: Croyland simply says 'a rumour was spread that the sons of Edward had died a violent death but it was uncertain how.' In other passages in Croyland and indeed in Mancini, they do not hesitate to point the finger at Richard or whoever else they think might have been responsible.

DR POLLARD: What they do is they most clearly state that Richard III deposed his nephew Edward V. They remain silent on the question . . .

MR DILLON: This trial is not directed to whether there was a usurpation but whether there was a murder.

DR POLLARD: Ah, but a usurpation therefore gave a reason for a murder.

MR DILLON: Well we'll see about that in a moment or two with another witness alas, much though I am enjoying facing you across this court-room.

Let me come to the poem, if I may please, which is a bit of Latin doggerel, the author not being identified. At the end of this passage of the continuation of the *Croyland Chronicle* it reads, 'Richard III was not content therewith,' – namely, Edward's fortune, carefully garnered during his years on the throne – 'but must destroy his brother's progeny' and you have indicated your understanding of that is 'bring the ruin of', because the Latin word which is used is *'opprimeret'*.

JUDGE: Would one find that in the papers?

MR DILLON: Alas no. Because your Lordship hasn't got a copy of the Latin any more than I have, but I have been given access to it. The passage in fact reads, if everybody will forgive my mispronunciation: *'Nisi fratres opprimeret proles'*. Now the verb *opprimere* can be used in the sense of putting down the cause of, or reducing to impotence or inactivity. Because what is being conveyed here is that Richard destroyed their inheritance, the children's, the Princes', inheritance. He destroyed their political, he destroyed their royal personality by his actions, it does not mean, or in any case does not necessarily mean, that he murdered them.

DR POLLARD: Yes that's a case that's been written in a very worthwhile book recently.

JUDGE: What do you think is the case?

DR POLLARD: What do I think is the case? I think this word has several possible different meanings and I think it is going to remain a matter of some dispute as to exactly what the author meant.

JUDGE: It's genuinely ambiguous?

DR POLLARD: It's a genuinely ambiguous word, yes.

MR DILLON: Has your Lordship got the poem and the few lines that preceded it?

JUDGE: No.

MR DILLON: I would only draw attention, if I may, that the few lines that preceded it read in the English translation, 'on taking into consideration the signs and badges of the conqueror and the conquered in our day, as well as those of the children of King Edward, whose cause in especial was avenged in this battle,' referring to Bosworth. Taking that alongside this piece of Latin doggerel, the meaning to be ascribed to it, I respectfully suggest, is as I have put it to you.

DR POLLARD: I think it's genuinely ambiguous. I don't think it necessarily means what you suggest.

MR DILLON: Very well. Then two things only: in relation to Croyland and in relation to Mancini. One of our troubles is that all the chroniclers are southerners or, like Mancini, are reporting the southern cause. There is not a single northern chronicler. One of the things that marks the whole of this period is the fear of the south of the barbarians or aliens from the north and the distrust from those of the north for those of the south. One of the things that one finds is the substantial prejudice running through Croyland, I respectfully suggest, of the southerner about the northerner. Can I read one passage to you?

My Lord it's page 509. If it's not included in the bundle which you have, during the adjournment I will ensure that you have it. Referring to the period after Henry has ascended the throne. While visiting York. . . .

JUDGE: What page is that?

MR DILLON: 509. The right hand side. Two thirds of the way down the page. Just before another Latin doggerel poem. This time the author says it's his, where he doesn't about the former one that we have looked at already.

Henry VII was visiting York and there was an uprising while he was there. The chronicle reports it in this way: 'Although by these means peace was graciously restored, still the rage of some of the malignants was not averted. But immediately after Easter sedition was set on foot by these ingrates in the north whence every evil takes its rise.'

DR POLLARD: Splendid stuff isn't it?

MR DILLON: Isn't it. And this even although the King was staying in those parts. I mean the impertinent northerners when the King is there, daring to rise. That's a fair extract because I can only use one.

DR POLLARD: That's very fair.

MR DILLON: The other I'd like to ask you about, if I may please, in relation to Mancini, as you have indicated he obtained his information from a number of different sources but clearly the Latin Genoese merchants and so on would be a fruitful one for him, particularly as he didn't speak English.

DR POLLARD: Not necessarily a lot of English. We don't know how much.

MR DILLON: A little. Never went out of London, clearly was closer to the court of Edward IV. No contact with Richard III. Not even a physical description of Richard. It's running throughout. Can I quote to you what another Italian said of the period, facing much the same sort of difficulties that Mancini did? 'I wish the people were plunged deep in the sea because of their lack of stability, for I feel like one going to the torture when I write about them. No one ever hears twice alike about English affairs.'* It's almost an up to date report I suppose.

JUDGE: This was another Italian.

MR DILLON: That's another Italian. Another Italian spy.

MR RUSSELL: Thank you Dr Pollard.

---

* The Italian cited by the barrister was a Milanese agent writing to his government in 1471. The letter is in the Milanese State Papers, and was quoted by C.A.J. Armstrong in *Some Examples of the Distribution and Speed of News in England at the time of the Wars of the Roses*, published in 1948.

Dr Starkey please.

MR RUSSELL: Dr Starkey, is your christian name David.

DR STARKEY: It is indeed and Robert too.

MR RUSSELL: What are your qualifications?

DR STARKEY: I am a doctor of philosophy in History, an expert in the Tudor court with an interest in the later fifteenth century.

MR RUSSELL: You have been listening no doubt to the evidence to date. Did you hear what Dr Pollard said about the pre-contract.

DR STARKEY: Yes. I agreed with everything that he said. It is clearly a concatenation of lies, rumour and absurdity but we can go very much further. It is not merely a concatenation of absurdity. It was a red herring and was known to be.

MR RUSSELL: Why?

DR STARKEY: Because succession wipes out illegitimacy as every other obstacle to the throne. Edward of course had succeeded, he was king, absolutely.

MR RUSSELL: On what basis.

DR STARKEY: By proclamation, by acceptance, by oaths of allegiance led by Richard himself and by the execution of acts of state and the royal signature appended thereto.

MR RUSSELL: So what you are saying then, quite simply, is that pre-contract doesn't arise because Edward V had acceded and therefore in law . . .

DR STARKEY: If you wish exact citation, in the sixteenth century Sergeant Plowden* describes accession as being 'like a very diamond, yea the philosopher's stone which wipeth out all blot'. And we have indeed not merely the theory, the practice. Queen Elizabeth of blessed memory, the descendant of so many of the people involved in our story this afternoon, was bastardized in 1536. She nevertheless ascended the throne unchallenged in 1588 and never thought to wipe out that bastardy because the very act of her accession did it for her.

MR RUSSELL: Yes thank you. Now . . .

MR DILLON: 1558.

DR STARKEY: 1558. The correction is most welcome sir.

MR DILLON: I hope to continue in the same vein sir!

DR STARKEY: A little more Irish logic would help us Mr Dillon.

---

* Sergeant Plowden was a mid-sixteenth-century lawyer.

Dr David Starkey

MR RUSSELL: By whom was the proclamation to which you attach, no doubt rightly, such importance?

DR STARKEY: By the council sir. By the council acting in its absolute capacity so to do. By the mayor of London, by Richard himself in the north and by every other authority in the country.

MR RUSSELL: Thank you.

Again do you agree with Dr Pollard that Mancini and Croyland are the most reliable contemporaneous chronicles?

DR STARKEY: Absolutely so. They had perfect access to information and complement each other.

MR RUSSELL: I only want to ask you one matter arising out of what they said and that was the murder of Hastings, as referred to by Mancini as we have heard. What interpretation do you place upon the reaction to the murder of Hastings?

DR STARKEY: It was a reaction, that was intended, to an act of unprecedented political terror. There is nothing in all the annals of the fifteenth century which parallels the conduct of Richard of Gloucester. A man is dragged actually from the cabinet table to instant execution. There is simply nothing like it. There are such executions after battle, as it were by the form of trial before the constable, but nothing like that, and it achieved the effect that was desired. Until that moment, everybody apart from Richard and Buckingham had tried to behave well; they had tried to follow the ordinary forms of law and decency, at that moment the political nation is stampeded, as Richard and Buckingham intended.

MR RUSSELL: Well now, may I come to what I really want to ask you about, Dr Starkey, and that is the later chroniclers, the sixteenth century Tudor chroniclers, of which you would tell us that the two best are More and Vergil.

DR STARKEY: I wouldn't call them chroniclers sir, if I may correct you, I would call them historians. This is the beginning of history, and it is something different.

MR RUSSELL: Let's deal with More first, I think he wrote a history of Richard III, in about 1513, so we are talking about thirty years after the event.

DR STARKEY: Yes, perhaps even finishing it as late, or rather breaking off, as late as 1521.

MR RUSSELL: Did he ever finish it.

DR STARKEY: He never finished it, it was broken off in 1521.

MR RUSSELL: Tell us a little about More quite shortly please.

DR STARKEY: More was a lawyer, an intellectual, a politician, a figure of international reputation, friend of Erasmus, eventually canonised, Henry's Lord Chancellor and 'the King's good servant, but God's first', in his own apt words.

MR RUSSELL: Now, he tells the story of which I outlined in my opening.

DR STARKEY: Indeed sir.

MR RUSSELL: I don't think I need repeat it, but just in a sentence: that Richard III had first of all asked Brackenbury to do the deed, Brackenbury refused and therefore Sir James Tyrell was sent, and he arranged the two servants to smother and bury them under the staircase and so on. It's been criticised, More, More's version, I think as an intellectual joke, a parody, leg pull and obviously invented, and so on. Do you place any reliance upon the More version of these events?

DR STARKEY: Yes, the criticisms of More on the whole are very small minds attacking a very big one, which is not an unusual experience. If we actually look at More's account, it corresponds precisely and in absolute detail with everything which is known of the inner machinery of the royal household. We have then Brackenbury having refused the deed, Richard fuming as he sits, as More puts it, at the draught. Namely on the privy, now this seems very extraordinary, because he's actually talking to somebody at the same time, but in those days as Montaigne* said, the higher you were the less privacy you had, even when you were sitting on the privy. The page is doing what any secret page either at the court of Edward IV or Henry VIII would have been expected to do, he is advising Richard – he says 'Outside there beyond the lavatory door, there is lying on a pallet mattress the man, Sir James Tyrell, who will do the deed for you', that is exactly what would have been happening. Tyrell as knight of the body would have been on the pallett outside the chamber door, the exact procedure is there. This is to be taken seriously.

MR RUSSELL: And so this is what More says – we haven't actually referred to it in my . . . and I haven't referred to it in my outline. But More discloses how while the King was on the draught, the privy, that he spoke to his page, and that his page suggested Sir James Tyrell and so on, and he was brought in from outside, and ordered to do the deed. . . .

DR STARKEY: This is an exact parallel as I've said, to a known court procedure, in periods like my own, when we have better documenta-

* Michel Montaigne – French humanist philosopher 1533–92.

tion, and also earlier ones like Edward IV, when the office of the groomship of the stool, is beginning to emerge, that is the king's lavatory attendant, was becoming the head of the inner royal household.

MR RUSSELL: You said this was the beginning of history, as distinct from chronicles, but in what manner did people write in those days, because again More's embellishments, and conversations, and interpolated speeches and so on have been criticised, as obviously having been invented.

DR STARKEY: I think we have to remember two things about how they worked. Nowadays when historians want to say that so and so existed in such a social context, they write an unbelievable, and I speak from experience, they write an unbelievably boring introduction about the social context of England when the man lived. Then, you did it much more interestingly, you put it in his own mouth, you input speeches there, and everybody knew there was this convention, there's no problem with it; moreover we as historians, not perhaps having the same hesitation about dealing with the past as lawyers, are able to distinguish truth from falsehood, in these matters, with very very few problems. Secondly, I think we should point out that there is a different approach too in terms of documentation. It is the beginning of history, these men were not writing with great piles of records, indexed nicely in front of them as we have now. They didn't have perpetual calenders as we do now, they got confused about dates, because in those days, very often you didn't actually date a document by the day of the month and the year, you used a saint's day, and there were in any case, three different years all going together.

MR RUSSELL: Dr Starkey what you're saying therefore is it's difficult to get the facts right and the date right and so on.

DR STARKEY: Yes, absolutely and mistakes are common. We see somebody like More, writing under immense pressure, telling us in *Utopia* that he had to snatch time to write from between meals and even from sleep and even from the marriage bed.

JUDGE: You mean pressure of time.

DR STARKEY: Pressure of time sir, and also great difficulty of sources; for us it's easy to be accurate, for them it was very difficult. If I may say so My Lord, even lawyers at that time, often got the dates of their statutes wrong, because reference to the rolls of parliament was very difficult.

JUDGE: Can even happen today.

DR STARKEY: I'm sure . . .

MR RUSSELL: I think in the opening lines to this part of the story, he uses the words, does More, 'hard that it be not true', and in the closing lines 'And thus I have learned of them that much knew, and had little cause to lie'. Would More have written in that way, if he didn't believe in the truth of his version?

DR STARKEY: No sir.

MR RUSSELL: It's suggested that, I think, or has been suggested, it may well be suggested today, I know not, that this is biased Tudor propaganda. Does that accord with your view?

DR STARKEY: I think there are three very simple things to be said: propaganda is always better if it's round the basis of truth; everything that More says is to be paralleled in detail in works written before the Tudor period; and finally if as we so often do, or some critics of More do say, 'we must not believe him, because he makes certain mistakes', that would mean simply sir, that we had no history, because there is no man yet who did not make a mistake somewhere.

MR RUSSELL: Was there any reason for More to have picked on an innocent Sir John Tyrell, and named him as a murderer in this account?

DR STARKEY: None whatsoever, nor an innocent Forest nor an innocent Dighton.

MR RUSSELL: Then finally, just a word or two about the other historian (I won't use the word chronicler) the other historian at that time, Polydore Vergil. Again he was an Italian I think, but came to England in the early part of the sixteenth century, 1502, and was commissioned by Henry VII to write a history of England.

DR STARKEY: That is correct.

MR RUSSELL: He gives an account very similar to More's, but in far less detail.

DR STARKEY: That is true.

MR RUSSELL: That would be a fair summary would it.

DR STARKEY: It would.

MR RUSSELL: And it's said of course, that the fact that he doesn't give the same detail as More underlines that More's detail is wrong. Do you accord with that view?

DR STARKEY: No, I think it's of a piece with the rest of the arguments of people who say that sort of thing, they haven't even bothered to count the number of pages. Polydore Vergil's entire account of the whole reign of Richard is only one quarter of the length of More's account of the first few months of it. Polydore Vergil is writing a gigantic history of England, going back from the days of Arthur to his own times. The reign of Richard III is an episode, so for artistic balance you do not have the same amount of detail, it's as simple as that.

MR RUSSELL: And finally do we find, I think, in the Fabyan chronicles* that of the gentleman of the city of London, who became Sheriff of London, does he report that 'it was common fame that Richard had the Princes put to secret death.'

DR STARKEY: He does indeed.

MR RUSSELL: And I think the *Chronicles of London*, as they are known (the reference being *Vitellius†*), that does record 'he also put to death the two children of King Edward, from which cause he lost the heart of the people.'

DR STARKEY: It does indeed sir.

JUDGE: What were the dates of those approximately?

DR STARKEY: They are essentially reminiscences sir, if I may My Lord, if I may interpolate. I do not necessarily put great reliance on them, but they certainly tell us what was happening in the city, they certainly tell us what men of some information thought, though not great.

JUDGE: But they were written in the Tudor period.

DR STARKEY: They were written indeed in the Tudor period by men alive at the time, and perhaps coloured by what I'm sure will now be called Tudor propaganda.

JUDGE: Yes, thank you.

MR DILLON: I thought I might say Tudor legend.

DR STARKEY: I'm sure you would sir, yes.

MR DILLON: Does that sound better to you?

DR STARKEY: It won't be the first time you've misused a word.

MR DILLON: I dare say.

DR STARKEY: Nor the last.

MR DILLON: Please help, does it sound better?

DR STARKEY: No.

MR DILLON: I see. Then if this small lawyer's mind may ask you some questions about the topics on which you have given evidence, Dr Stacey.

---

* *The New Chronicles of England and France* by Robert Fabyan, a city alderman, published after his death in 1513.

† *Chronicles of London*, known as *Vitellius A XVI*, after their Cottonian Library shelf number. They probably date from the early part of Henry VII's reign.

DR STARKEY: Starkey.

MR DILLON: Thank you. You have been led to say that the account given by Polydore Vergil and More, is similar.

DR STARKEY: There are similar elements.

MR DILLON: Yes, of course. May I simply draw attention, so that the jury may follow, to what could be said to be substantial differences between the two.

DR STARKEY: But of course.

MR DILLON: The Tyrell confession which is referred to in More – is not referred to in Vergil at all.

DR STARKEY: Quite.

MR DILLON: Tyrell is described as being forced to do the King's commandment, and riding sorrowfully from York to London, whereas in fact More doesn't describe him riding in that way at all. And indeed More says that he travelled from Warwick. The role of the page, never mind the privy, because that's left out as well, but the role of the page, of Green, of Forest, and of Dighton, are all omitted from Vergil. But perhaps more important simply concentrating on the essential features, if I may with you please, Dr Starkey, Vergil finishes his account saying, with what kind of death these seely, meaning innocent, children were executed, it was not certainly known. Well then with that in mind I'll ask you, if I may, some questions about Tyrell in particular, concentrating just on that aspect, and perhaps the withered arm part of More. I must ask one question about the succession to get that out of the way. I would respectfully accept everything that you have said about succession wiping out illegitimacy, if you were to say that it was the annointing and the recognition ceremony within the coronation which would wipe out all past evils.

DR STARKEY: And I think you would be wrong.

MR DILLON: May I finish the question.

DR STARKEY: No, sir, because I think it is founded on completely false premise. I take it therefore –

MR DILLON: If you please.

DR STARKEY: – that you do not recognise the succession of Edward VIII who was not crowned.

MR DILLON: If you please.

DR STARKEY: The coronation has never played the role that you are attributing to it.

JUDGE: I think if you allow counsel –

DR STARKEY: I will sir. I'm sorry, My Lord.

JUDGE: – to complete the question.

MR DILLON: I will pass on, because time presses upon me, at any rate.

DR STARKEY: Facts too.

MR DILLON: Help me please about the Duke of Buckingham, I would be right in thinking, and indeed the jury can see for themselves from the little chart that has been drawn up, that the Duke of Buckingham, had indeed himself a good claim to the throne.

DR STARKEY: A passable one.

MR DILLON: He was directly descended through the Duke of Gloucester, Thomas of Woodstock, was he not?

DR STARKEY: Yes.

MR DILLON: Could also claim descent from John of Gaunt, but can I leave that on one side entirely for the moment. In addition in 1474, Buckingham had obtained the right to use the heraldic device of Woodstock, linking him directly to that descent. Buckingham was a very dark and shadowy figure, not a very attractive man, very well spoken, very plausible, with his eyes very much on the throne for himself, do you agree with that?

DR STARKEY: It is, yes I do.

MR DILLON: Vergil reports of him, and I take this extract only as one, by way of an example, 'that the multitude said that the Duke did the less persuade Richard of Gloucester from usurping the throne, by the means of so many mischievous deeds, with the intent that he Richard afterwards being hated both of God and man, might be expelled from the same, so that himself Buckingham called by the Commons to that dignity where onto he aspired by all means possible.' And there were reports from More and from others of his . . .

DR STARKEY: Are we believing More at this point sir?

MR DILLON: No, I'm just asking the question if I may, please.

DR STARKEY: The statement has gone on so long I am now entirely unclear as to the question.

MR DILLON: There are reports, are there not, from others as well, of his disliking Richard's gaining the crown rather than himself.

DR STARKEY: Retrospectively, yes.

MR DILLON: Buckingham of course could not gain the throne if the Princes remained alive. Can I establish with you some facts, as to dates please. The coronation took place on 9th July 1483.

DR STARKEY: Unlike you I have not, I'm afraid, refreshed my memory precisely. Let's have a look shall we.

MR DILLON: Let's take that as an accepted date, and it can be corrected if I have mis-stated.

DR STARKEY: We now both have our sheets of information, in front of us.

MR DILLON: No, I have not your sheet of information, never mind. The 6th July I am corrected from behind. Shortly after that date, Richard set out with his wife the Queen, on a kind of royal progress, through Windsor, Oxford, to Gloucester where he arrived by 29th July, and stayed till the 2nd August, is that right?

DR STARKEY: You're telling me.

MR DILLON: I'm asking a question.

DR STARKEY: I'm sorry I do not have this information at my fingertips, being a modern historian I am used to using, as it were, little things in books, as you did to put it together. Carry on.

MR DILLON: Yes, let's assume that I'm correct, if I may.

DR STARKEY: It's dangerous, but I will.

MR DILLON: Very well, then I won't trouble with the rest of that line of questioning. Let me just ask you something then please about More. We concentrate on Tyrell, because it is said by More, who is a lawyer, as you pointed out, that Tyrell upon his accusation of treason, was 'examined and confessed in the manner above written, but whither the bodies were removed they' because the passage refers to both Tyrell and Dighton, 'could nothing tell.'

JUDGE: Who are you quoting from there?

MR DILLON: That's from More, page 84.

DR STARKEY: He is using I'm afraid a paperback edition, the thing is here.

MR DILLON: I was using one that I've obtained from a library, published in 1883, I'm afraid.

DR STARKEY: It's very out of date, I'm sorry, the standard is the one before me, would you like to establish . . .

JUDGE: It matters not. What are the words.

MR DILLON: I'm so sorry to use an edition which is out of date. The words are 'Tyrell and Dighton were examined and confessed in the manner above written, relating to the death of the Princes, but whither the bodies were removed, they could nothing tell.' On the following page, More recites that Dighton, is still walking free, I forget the exact words, but he'll catch his just deserts in the end, something to that effect.

DR STARKEY: True.

MR DILLON: 'Walketh yet on alive.' 'Alive' but it finishes with somebody will catch up with him in the end.

MR RUSSELL: 'A good possibility he will be hanged ere he died.'

MR DILLON: 'Ere, he died', now that's written in 1513.

DR STARKEY: Probably '21 sir, if you use a more recent edition, you would have seen that the likely terminal date is the execution of Buckingham's son in 1521 at which time More wrote a work which cites large passages of this, and a deeply serious one.

MR DILLON: Then you make my point even more valid. It's not as I was thinking, nine years after the time of the trial of Tyrell for treason, it's even longer than that, eighteen or nineteen years after the trial for treason. But Dighton was never tried.

DR STARKEY: Why should he have been. The treason on which Tyrell was arraigned was not the treason of the murder of the Princes in the Tower.

MR DILLON: Can you confirm to me please that Dighton was not tried for treason?

DR STARKEY: There is no evidence of the fact. Tyrell was not tried on this issue sir. Tyrell was tried not on the grounds of that confession, but because of his alliance with the De la Poles. Therefore I'm afraid you're confusing the issue utterly, and not for the first time.

MR DILLON: Thank you so much Mr Starkey.

DR STARKEY: Dr Starkey.

MR DILLON: I'm so sorry Dr Starkey, I shan't ask any further questions.

MR RUSSELL: Yes, thank you Dr Starkey.

My Lord, as I indicated, that is my last witness, that is the case for the prosecution.

JUDGE: Much obliged thank you.

MR DILLON: If your Lordship please, members of the jury it now falls for me to open the case on behalf of the defence. In doing so, I am entitled to adopt the same course as Mr Russell has, and to explain to you, not at length, but at any rate in some detail, the evidence that I am proposing to call. I do not propose to do so. I think it's very much better that you hear the evidence direct from the witnesses. The nature of their evidence, however, I will indicate to you very shortly. Really we have one contention only to lay before you, namely that two views can be taken on every point that is raised by the prosecution. Those are honestly held views, and you'll hear them from the

Mr Dillon, the defence barrister

witnesses that I shall call. And in due course I shall respectfully suggest to you, that they are valid views, as I say it's better that you hear those from them, than from me. I'm going to call three witnesses in all: Lady Wedgwood who is an art historian, who will show you how quickly, not Tudor propaganda, or Tudor legend, but Tudor tradition, as it eventually became, painted in black and white only, Richard III wholly black, and Henry VII wholly white. How that was created in her field, how persuasively it was presented, and how persistently its echoes remain even to today.

I shall then call an archivist, to deal with the question of the pre-contract between Edward IV and Eleanor Butler. She will tell you that it is, in her view, despite what Dr Pollard told us, that it raised a real issue then, and still indeed does today. Now here evidence I think I can take fairly shortly, because there is a substantial degree of agreement about the framework within which that evidence is given, the dispute, the confrontation, whatever is the right word to use, lying between those who believe that it was a claim validly made, and those who do not. As we attach, on this side of the court, significance to the fact that it was Henry VII himself who prevented any examination into Stillington's claim, after he had come to the throne.

Now the third witness that I shall call is Mr Potter, who is Chairman of the Richard III Society, who will deal with Richard the man, presenting a rather different picture from that which was presented by the first of my friend's witnesses, who will speak of course of the pressures upon Richard arising at the time, and this inevitable struggle for power which Edward IV left behind him, having allowed the Woodvilles to assume as much power in the way that you have been told, who will explain why it was that Richard acted as he did, why it may have been. Because we do not claim our witnesses to be versed with the answers to all questions at all, they will not speak anything like as positively as those who have been called by my friend. He will speak also of Buckingham, that rather dark mysterious double dealer, of the period. Would you bear in mind please, that you are considering a period only between April, in effect, and August of 1483 – the whole of Richard's life prior to that time, not in the company of Buckingham, and the whole of his life after that time, not in the company of Buckingham. His behaviour is criticised only within that short space of time while Buckingham too is upon the scene. May I make it absolutely clear, so there is no misunderstanding from the start, that our case does not depend upon proving that Buckingham was the culprit, it's not the

Lady Wedgwood under examination by Mr Dillon

duty in any criminal trial, and will not be our duty here in this. What we simply say is that there is too little hard evidence to come to a firm conclusion even on a balance of probabilities. That it is to say even twisting the scale and onus of proof which is required, the degree of proof which is required in our courts, to match in the circumstances that we face here, seeking to mount a trial some five hundred years after the events themselves took place. Now having said that I will go straight into calling the evidence, calling first of all Lady Wedgwood please.

MR DILLON: Your Lordship has I hope, and the jury has I hope as well, a bundle which is marked in a little brown envelope, 'photo packet three: portraits'. It's not very easy to get the contents out. When you have, you will find on the top what appears in the photograph to be a line drawing, which this witness will be referring to.

Lady Wedgwood, you're a Fellow of the Society of Antiquaries, and principally, apart from lecturing and writing extensively on your subject – which is that of an art historian I think –

LADY WEDGWOOD: Medieval art historian.

MR DILLON: – specialising in the medieval period, was responsible for mounting the exhibition on Richard III in the National Portrait Gallery in 1973.

LADY WEDGWOOD: That is correct.

MR DILLON: I think then you did assemble almost all the known portraits of Richard III, although curiously enough even some more have come to light since then.

LADY WEDGWOOD: Indeed. I have note then of over twenty, the total is rising towards thirty, and others may yet emerge. But this is a question of duplicates, rather than originals.

MR DILLON: I'll come onto that in a moment. I think included in the exhibition were many letters and manuscripts, some in Richard III's own hand, and many artefacts of the period and of the personalities that we are concerned with.

I would like to read to you, if I may, from my old edition of Sir Thomas More his description of Richard III which is passed down into posterity. Starting off by saying that he is less than Edward, who preceded him, as king, it goes on to say 'Little of stature, ill-featured of limbs, crook backed [means humped backed], his left shoulder much higher than his right, hard favoured of visage, and such as in the states called warly . . .' I'm not quite sure what 'warly' means, but

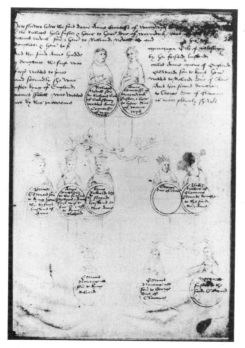

ITEM 1. Neville family tree from the Beauchamp Pageant. Richard is third in on the second row

ITEM 2. Detail from the Beauchamp Pageant. Richard is on the right, in the centre is his wife Anne Neville and on the left is her first husband

its clearly not a compliment by the sound of it. First of all, is that supported by the contemporary paintings or the contemporary accounts?

JUDGE: Crooked-back and hard what did you say?

MR DILLON: Hard faced of visage. Little of stature, and hard backed, ill featured of limbs; More goes on later to say he'd got a withered arm, any truth in that?

LADY WEDGWOOD: There is no contemporary evidence that he had a withered arm from any visual sources. That he was considerably shorter than his brother, Edward, and of quite a different cast of feature, could very well be demonstrated . . .

MR DILLON: Crook-backed, humped-back?

LADY WEDGWOOD: The first record of that is a written one, where it is accepted that there was some disparity in shoulders.

MR DILLON: Ah, that's a different kettle of fish, many of us have got one shoulder slightly higher than the other, or one slightly larger than the other, but humped-backed.

LADY WEDGWOOD: That is, I claim, an exaggeration.

MR DILLON: Then can I ask you to look at the contemporary portraits. Is that the first that we have in the bundle before the jury?

LADY WEDGWOOD: The image you have, the black and white one like this, is the one definite image of Richard, made during his reign, almost certainly drawn by somebody who had seen him. And the figure in question is this one, that is the third in on the second row, this is the genealogical tree of his wife, Anne Neville and it gives her parents, Warwick the Kingmaker, the George Duke of Clarence with her sister, and with her two husbands.

MR DILLON: Well I needn't go into the others, we can concentrate on Richard III.

LADY WEDGWOOD: This one.

MR DILLON: The second that we've got is an enlargement of the three to which you have drawn attention. Richard being on the right hand side I think.

LADY WEDGWOOD: Indeed.

MR DILLON: Again, any evidence there of deformity?

LADY WEDGWOOD: Certainly not, nothing of the kind is conveyed, though the short face perhaps which is a contrast to his brother, could be pointed out.

MR DILLON: We are now going to turn to number three, which is a coloured print, and in fact a picture which is in possession of your society.

ITEM 3. The Society of Antiquaries portrait of Richard III. 'This painting which suggests no deformity or exaggeration of any kind is probably the earliest known copy of a lost original'

ITEM 4. Portrait from the Royal Collection at Windsor. 'The last link of the chain, his collar, is painted in a different hand, more clumsily than the other, and the uppermost part of the painting of his shoulder line is exaggerated'

Portrait in the collection of Lord
Stafford

From the National Portrait
Gallery, London

ITEM 5. Four portraits of
Richard III

In the collection of the Duke of Northumberland

From the collection of the Duke of Leeds, now at the National Portrait Gallery, Montacute

ITEM 5. Four portraits of Richard III

LADY WEDGWOOD: The Society of Antiquaries.

MR DILLON: Is that a faithful portrait of Richard as he appeared in life, prior to his death on Bosworth Field?

LADY WEDGWOOD: It is completely compatible with the photos you have already seen, and the contemporary drawing. This painting, which suggests no deformity or exaggeration of any kind, is probably the earliest known copy of a lost original, it was in the Paston family until the eighteenth century, it shows no deformity or nothing special at all.

MR DILLON: Well then I'm going to go on to number four, if I may. This is a portrait taken from the Royal collection of Windsor, we cannot alas show it, but under X-ray is it possible to demonstrate that the right shoulder in fact has been lifted?*

LADY WEDGWOOD: This is the case, Mr Dillon, in fact the last link of the chain, his collar, is painted in a different hand, more clumsily than the other, and the uppermost part of the painting of his shoulder line is exaggerated. There is a little bit of alteration there, which has made the point of a very definitely different shoulder, this one slopes down. This picture is somewhere around 1530, and once more as near as we had to an original after the other one.

JUDGE: You mean, by examination you can show some paint added at a different period.

LADY WEDGWOOD: Yes, the original shoulder line, My Lord, runs there.

MR DILLON: There has been a deliberate alteration to the right shoulder.

LADY WEDGWOOD: And it has been, and it is, also suggested that the eyes have been made more narrow.

MR DILLON: The face looks to be a good deal more lined too, in this and subsequent portraits we are going to look at, than the original.

LADY WEDGWOOD: Indeed, he was only in his early thirties, when he died.

MR DILLON: Thirty one at the time of the accession to the throne. Well, then there's a group of others, because one passes on to copies of copies of copies, does one not, and the next three, four that the jury have got in their bundle, simply continue to reproduce the errors, which one has seen, the deliberate errors that one has seen in the one to which you have now drawn attention.

LADY WEDGWOOD: This is in the Stafford collection, not before the 1550s, this one in the National Portrait Gallery, not before the 1590s, and this one Duke of Northumberland, probably 1600 maybe 1620, and the last one the Duke of Leeds, now at Montacute 1600–1620 again.

---

* In fact the disparity showed up more clearly without X-rays.

MR DILLON: I need not dwell upon those, because the point is the same, it is the distorted image which has been copied. I think there is an outstanding example which you have.

LADY WEDGWOOD: Yes.

MR DILLON: It's the portrait of Richard with the broken sword.

LADY WEDGWOOD: This is, you might say, an independent witness, evidently the same face, clearly a propaganda picture.

MR DILLON: Could you hold it for one moment, so his Lordship can see, and my friend.

LADY WEDGWOOD: There you will see he is holding a broken sword, that in itself suggests that it was clearly posthumous, but if you look at an image, in examining it you will see that it has been altered in itself.

MR DILLON: Now what you are holding is now a black and white portrait.

LADY WEDGWOOD: This is the infra-red photograph of it, where you can see there have been two alterations. It was originally painted with a very exaggerated left shoulder, this was —

MR DILLON: Can I stop you there.

LADY WEDGWOOD: Yes.

MR DILLON: Does that give the appearance of the hump-back?

LADY WEDGWOOD: Indeed sir, the other shoulder is somewhere down here.

MR DILLON: It's been dropped, could you point it in my direction for one moment.

LADY WEDGWOOD: This very considerable exaggeration here, very low shoulder there, but that has been altered to make it more normal – it was originally painted, My Lord, with a very deformed left arm, of which the cuff came to here, and the line went there.

MR DILLON: Oh that's to give the appearance of the withered left arm. Could you hold that round to point to the jury please.

LADY WEDGWOOD: You can see the original line of the arm was there, right here, so that it was sort of the fraction of the proper length, but it was then altered to suggest a long arm, matching this one, which would have been out of the picture. This picture has been in known hands since 1783, and therefore . . .

MR DILLON: I'm going to stop you. Forgive me because it becomes fascinating to know when the alteration was made to paint out the hump or reduce it.

LADY WEDGWOOD: Without the hump.

MR DILLON: And to paint out the withered arm.

LADY WEDGWOOD: Indeed.

ITEM 6. Portrait of Richard with a broken sword, from the collection of the Society of Antiquaries

ITEM 7. Infra-red photograph of Richard with a broken sword showing
that 'it was originally painted with a very exaggerated left shoulder . . .
and a very deformed left arm'

MR DILLON: But we're not here to examine that, expert though I know you are. What I would like to ask, is that when one thinks of – as one is bound to I think in this context – when one talks of Richard III, Sir Laurence Olivier's portrait of him, while that may be absolutely faithful to Shakespeare, is it a true reproduction of what Richard III himself was like?

LADY WEDGWOOD: I think one can say it stands in the relationship to the truth, as the latest of those portraits does.

MR DILLON: Now that kind of manipulation, and I use the word deliberately, is that also found in some of the written records about Richard III?

LADY WEDGWOOD: Undoubtedly.

MR DILLON: Now very briefly . . .

JUDGE: Now if these were manipulations where would they be exhibited? Where would people see them, learn about them; where would the propaganda effect be achieved? They were all in private collections were they?

LADY WEDGWOOD: Well My Lord, the chief private collection in question was always the Royal Collection.

JUDGE: I see.

LADY WEDGWOOD: And the most important of these portraits, the one that was actually altered, was in the Royal Collection.

MR DILLON: Well then I am going to deal with this without producing any more exhibits, particularly by way of two questions, if I may. Was one of the historians of the period, a recorder for the Warwick family called John Rous?

LADY WEDGWOOD: Yes.

MR DILLON: Who wrote what is now known by experts in the field, as the *Rous Roll*.

LADY WEDGWOOD: Two *Rous Rolls* in fact.

MR DILLON: The roll which we can call the York one, that came into existence before the death of Richard III, and was made during his reign, are there flattering references to Richard?

LADY WEDGWOOD: Indeed there is a very extensive quotation – may I give you the words?

MR DILLON: · No, because I am going to stop you I'm afraid. Immediately after Richard died on the field at Bosworth, what did Rous do with that roll?

LADY WEDGWOOD: He had already said goodbye to it, it was I'm convinced in royal hands. He'd I'm sure made if for the Queen, and he had though, in his hands, a second roll, which was in Latin, and this one he feverishly cut up, to alter, to turn its coat. And it is that cutting up that is still plain. That one also survives, they are both extant, that one is the College of Arms. He cut out the first image of Richard, with his brother Edward, and inserted an Edward III, which was safe. He . . .

MR DILLON: In modern parlance, I'm going to interrupt I'm afraid, in modern parlance is this called editing?

LADY WEDGWOOD: Well if you use scissors sir, yes, it is editing. And in the second case, he cut the division between Anne and her husband, he inserted her first husband, son of Henry VI, with a big panegyric there, and for Richard he expunged all the praise, and just put 'unhappy husband'.

MR DILLON: Thank you.

JUDGE: He doctored it, according to what you are saying.

LADY WEDGWOOD: Indeed.

MR RUSSELL: Lady Wedgwood I think only this, if we can just summarise your evidence about the portraits and see how relevant they are to the issue which this jury has to understand. What you're really saying, it appears that – and you have shown to us, and it was highly interesting if I may say so – it appears that after the event, Richard was made to appear more attractive, unattractive rather, than he had been portrayed previously.

LADY WEDGWOOD: Indeed.

MR RUSSELL: And you have shown us that, related to the raising or dropping of a shoulder, and the narrowing of eyes.

LADY WEDGWOOD: Indeed.

MR RUSSELL: That, with the very greatest of respect, that doesn't really help to decide whether he killed the Princes or not, does it?

LADY WEDGWOOD: I think if you can see that the manipulation of evidence is taken so far that a picture in the royal hands has to go, you might say, to the surgeon, then they are very determined to alter the material.

MR RUSSELL: Yes but it doesn't, again with respect, it doesn't really answer my question, does it? It doesn't help us, it doesn't help this jury to decide whether or not at the end of July or beginning of August of 1483, that Richard instructed someone to murder the two boys in the Tower.

LADY WEDGWOOD: This is only contemporary evidence of his appearance, and . . .

Miss Anne Sutton

MR RUSSELL: And indeed what those pictures show in effect is this, is it not, that those that were responsible for those alterations, might have thought and genuinely thought, that he was a murderer and a wicked man, and therefore portrayed him in an unattractive way. That's one answer isn't it?

LADY WEDGWOOD: Indeed.

MR RUSSELL: Yes, thank you very much.

MR DILLON: Thank you very much Lady Wedgwood.
Miss Sutton please.

MR DILLON: Miss Sutton I think you are an archivist employed by one of the city companies.

MISS SUTTON: I am.

MR DILLON: Specialising in the records that you keep from the late fifteenth century, the period that the jury are particularly concerned with.

MISS SUTTON: That's my personal interest, yes.

MR DILLON: A fellow again of the Society of Antiquaries.

MISS SUTTON: Yes.

MR DILLON: I think the author jointly of a fairly monumental work, if you'll forgive me so describing it, on the coronation of Richard III.

MISS SUTTON: Yes.

MR DILLON: Editor of the *Ricardian*, which is a publication of the Richard III Society, I think.

MISS SUTTON: Yes.

MR DILLON: And to have studied the question of the pre-contract, in particularly being familiar with a work which sounds very intimidating from Chicago University, Professor Helmholtz, entitled *Marriage Litigation in Medieval England*, which is published by the Cambridge University Press in 1975.

MISS SUTTON: Yes.

MR DILLON: Now with your knowledge of the period, of Richard III, and of the pre-contract, can I ask you two flat questions. It's been described – this question of the pre-contract – as being simply a pretext used by Richard to seize the throne for himself. Do you agree with that assessment?

MISS SUTTON: No.

MR DILLON: It has been described by one of the witnesses, and I hope I have the language right, as a red-herring, in fact, do you agree with that?

MISS SUTTON: No, it's the crux of the matter.

MR DILLON: What is not known by anybody, despite all the researches, is the date upon which Bishop Stillington might have mentioned the question of the pre-contract marriage, of Edward IV to Eleanor Butler.

MISS SUTTON: No, we can only speculate on that.

MR DILLON: But upon the basis that it was done as reported in Croyland, that this was a private marriage, clandestine and therefore not celebrated in public, not necessarily celebrated in church, not celebrated, particularly importantly I think, with the publication of banns, would that have been a valid ground for objecting to the validity of the marriage between Edward and Elizabeth Woodville subsequently?

MISS SUTTON: Yes.

MR DILLON: And inevitably leading then to the bastardisation of the children.

MISS SUTTON: Yes, the two things together.

MR DILLON: I need not ask you any of the details about it, save I think this: was adultery taken very seriously in fact in medieval times?

MISS SUTTON: Oh yes, it was a heinous crime.

MR DILLON: When there was a question of succession or inheritance raised?

MISS SUTTON: Yes, undoubtedly.

MR DILLON: Then I'm going to go on to this question please as it's suggested that parliament was not a suitable place to pronounce upon it, as parliament did, in the *Titulus Regius*, and Dr Pollard gave us the benefit of his view about the examples taken from Tudor times, relating to Elizabeth I and so on, do you remember?

MISS SUTTON: Strictly speaking the matter of the marriage and the pre-contract, the clandestine marriage and the pre-contract together, should have gone before an ecclesiastical court. The *Titulus Regius* did in fact mention this. It acknowledged this in a sense by emphasising the notoriety of the known two facts; that is to say the notoriety of the pre-contract with Eleanor Butler, and the notoriety of the clandestine marriage to Elizabeth Woodville. It is the two things together that are important. Not the pre-contract by itself.

MR DILLON: I follow.

MISS SUTTON: Once these are established as notorious, then the onus upon bringing the case was placed upon the children.

MR DILLON: I see – if there was to be a challenge of the matter, do you mean?

MISS SUTTON: Yes.

MR DILLON: I follow. Would it have been appropriate then – given the state of the law at that time, not yet settled, still in a matter of flux – appropriate for parliament to deal with it in the *Titulus Regius*.

MISS SUTTON: Yes, parliament at that time did in a sense pronounce, or rather confirm or ratify the individual king who was displacing another – that individual king's own personal claim to the throne – usually based in some way or other on the normal means of accession to the throne. Parliament just agreed, fundamentally.

JUDGE: How far was parliament a free parliament in regards its relationship with the king, could the king dictate to parliament – it wasn't the parliament of 1984 was it.

MISS SUTTON: No, it would accept in this instance what the king told it, yes.

JUDGE: Yes, yes, thank you.

MISS SUTTON: As indeed it had done with all the other kings who had displaced others in the fifteenth century.

MR DILLON: Indeed there was a petition from parliament to Richard to take the crown, prior to his coronation. Not parliament as assembled because not all the members were there.

MISS SUTTON: 'The three estates' it was called.

MR DILLON: Then the other matter I'd like to ask you about if I may please, is simply this, relating to the pre-contract; it is said by Dr Starkey that once proclamation had been made of Edward the Prince as King Edward V, then all questions of illegitimacy would have been wiped out. Do you agree with that view?

MISS SUTTON: Well I think it's true of Dr Starkey's period, but he is forgetting the reign of Henry VIII and the great increase of the theory of the absolute king. So the situation is entirely different in 1483.

MR DILLON: What in your view would have had to have happened, for illegitimacy like this to have been wiped out – the coronation itself?

MISS SUTTON: Yes, the act of recognition, the act of annointing and the act of coronation in that order.

MR DILLON: Well now the act of recognition is when the archbishop having crowned, annointed, given the orb and the sceptre I think, calls upon the lords assembled . . .

MISS SUTTON: Yes, it in fact precedes all of the other ceremonies.

MR DILLON: I am much obliged, quite right. And is part of the coronation service which survives even to today.

MISS SUTTON: Yes.

MR DILLON: Very well, then the only other matter that I'd like to ask about, please, is about Richard the Law Giver. We have not heard very much about Richard. I'll be asking Mr Potter after the adjournement about it. But have you looked at the statutes that he introduced during his period as king?

MISS SUTTON: Yes, I know them well.

MR DILLON: Sir Frances Bacon later commented, and no-one in this court I think will quarrel with the views of Sir Francis Bacon, that he was 'a good law maker', his laws were designed 'for the ease and the solace of the common people'. Is that a view that you would agree with?

MISS SUTTON: Oh yes, there are six statutes in particular that reflect this – I can pick out two now, there is the statute against benevolences, benevolences were . . .

MR DILLON: Forced taxation.

MISS SUTTON: Yes, gifts to the king without the free consent of his people, and Edward IV . . .

MR DILLON: Well that's a good definition of taxation I think in fact.

MISS SUTTON: But it was generally held in the Middle Ages, as indeed it is held now, that the people freely consent to taxation and to loans . . .

MR DILLON: That's what we're all supposed to do.

MISS SUTTON: By Richard's abolishing of benevolences, he is endorsing that idea.

MR DILLON: Just stay there. I won't trouble about the other one.

MR RUSSELL: Miss Sutton, in respect of the bastardisation of the two Princes, there were apparently two plans here in Richard's mind. Firstly, to suggest that Edward IV, the father of the Princes was a bastard and secondly that the Princes were, because of the pre-contract.

MISS SUTTON: I don't agree. We only have the chronicler's word for that. To my mind it's far more that they got it mixed up. They were confused by what was presented to them and therefore they fell back on the old story of Edward being a bastard because they couldn't comprehend the rather complicated canon law that came into play to make the Princes illegitimate.

MR RUSSELL: But in fact the chroniclers do say that there was a suggestion that Edward IV himself was a bastard because he had been conceived in adultery.

MISS SUTTON: Edward IV conceived in adultery? Yes, well that's an old story but I don't see how . . .

MR RUSSELL: That is what has been reported and failed to be mentioned thereafter and was completely dropped if the chroniclers are right.

MISS SUTTON: Yes, I don't think the chroniclers are right. I think they're confused.

MR RUSSELL: Now in relation to the pre-contract itself, that was done with indecent haste, wasn't it?

MISS SUTTON: How do you mean?

MR RUSSELL: Well, I, I mean this: Prince Richard was removed from sanctuary on 16th June upon the basis that he was going to attend his older brother, the King's coronation a few days later. Within five days of that or six days, I think it was 22nd June, Dr Shaw was preaching the bastardisation of the Princes from the pulpit at St Paul's Cross.

MISS SUTTON: What is indecently hurried about that?

MR RUSSELL: Well Miss Sutton, it came very quickly if one moment the Prince was to be crowned King and the next moment out of the blue it's said they are bastards upon the word of Bishop Stillington.

MISS SUTTON: Yes, yes that that's how it happened. I don't think we can argue with that. But I don't . . .

MR RUSSELL: And, and because of the indecent hurry it was accepted and it did not go through the normal process of the courts, did it.

MISS SUTTON: They didn't have an ecclesiastical court, no.

MR RUSSELL: Precisely. And strictly speaking I think, I quote you from your evidence in chief, strictly speaking that is what would have happened.

MISS SUTTON: You could equally argue that an ecclesiastical court on the canonical law, legal evidence would have had to have found for Richard.

MR RUSSELL: Well you can argue that, but the whole point is, Miss Sutton, that the ecclesiastical court was never given the opportunity so to do. That's the fact isn't it?

MISS SUTTON: No – yes – you're into the realm of political expediency now.

MR RUSSELL: No I'm not, with the greatest respect, into the realm of political expediency. I'm into the realm of the law. The law at that time said that an ecclesiastical court should have resolved the question as to whether or not there was a proved pre-contract and that would have meant Stillington giving evidence and being examined upon it and that never happened, did it.

MISS SUTTON: No, not at that point.

MR RUSSELL: What happened was that it was presented to the Lords at that time, the Lords not in parliament but the Lords in an assembly in London to which they had come from various parts of the country for the coronation. And it didn't, it didn't come before parliament until the following January, did it.

MISS SUTTON: No.

MR RUSSELL: And do you accept or not what Mancini said about this, and that the only reason why the Lords accepted it was because they'd seen what happened to Hastings, they'd seen the unholy alliance between Richard and Buckingham, they had realised that the multitude of troops from the north were at the gates of London and they were frightened.

JUDGE: They were intimidated, is that it, do you agree with that?

MISS SUTTON: That's one way of looking at it but it doesn't alter the fact that the pre-contract was a valid moral reason for Richard to take the throne.

MR RUSSELL: If it was a valid pre-contract, but that begs the question, doesn't it Miss Sutton. I'm suggesting to you that Dr Pollard is right when he says the pre-contract was in fact a trumped up pretext and trumped up in haste over a few days.

MISS SUTTON: Yes, I don't believe it was trumped up.

JUDGE: You'd describe it indeed as the crux of the matter.

MISS SUTTON: Yes.

JUDGE: Why do you say that?

MISS SUTTON: Because it gave Richard a genuine claim to the throne, a moral claim to the throne, as well as the political reasons to make him secure.

MR RUSSELL: And the evidence of Stillington, and it was only on the evidence of Stillington, wasn't it?

MISS SUTTON: Oh yes.

MR RUSSELL: Yes, came at a very opportune moment, at the very time that he wanted an excuse to take the crown.

JUDGE: May I ask how came it that Stillington took this upon himself to make this pronouncement?

MISS SUTTON: He was a canon lawyer, he could make the connection between the fact of the pre-contract and the clandestine second marriage.

MR RUSSELL: Miss Sutton, am I not right in saying that the suggestion was that Stillington had been the witness to the pre-contract?

MISS SUTTON: There is that suggestion, that, that could . . .

MR RUSSELL: I'm not suggesting that it's necessarily true . . .

MISS SUTTON: No.

MR RUSSELL: But in answer to what His Lordship says, I think there is a suggestion, I forget now where it comes, but that Stillington was the person who was the witness to the pre-contract and only he and Eleanor Butler and Edward IV knew about it and the other two parties Eleanor and Edward IV by then were dead.*

MISS SUTTON: That is found, yes.

MR RUSSELL: So here was one witness to say this about something about which silence had been kept over a period of what, fifteen years?

MISS SUTTON: In, in canon law, you didn't need more than that because you acted on the presumption of truth.

MR RUSSELL: It might have been very suspect though and indeed as I suggest it is.

MISS SUTTON: If people generally accepted it to be true that was more important than any evidence that could be presented in a court of law under canon law as they understood it.

MR RUSSELL: But the difficulty, the difficulty was of course that people didn't generally believe it was true and we get that from Mancini as well, don't we; 'the corrupt preachers' and the colour for the usurpation from Croyland.

MISS SUTTON: That's only one chronicler.

MR RUSSELL: And Croyland, the colour for the usurpation.

MISS SUTTON: Two chroniclers.

MR RUSSELL: And Mancini makes it clear that the general belief at the time was that this was not a true contract.

MISS SUTTON: Yes, it's still the words of two men.

MR RUSSELL: Better than the word of one, Miss Sutton, Bishop Stillington. In all events, if we face this practically, did it really matter in any event, because the fact that there may have been a pre-contract, the fact that the children may have been bastards? That could so easily have been reversed by parliament. And indeed was.

MISS SUTTON: It could have been.

---

* Philippe de Commynes in his *Memoires* says, 'The Bishop discovered to the Duke of Gloucester that his brother King Edward had been formerly in love with a beautiful young lady, and had promised her marriage, upon the condition he might lie with her; the lady consented, and, as the bishop affirmed, he married them when nobody was present but they two and himself. His fortune depending upon the court, he did not discover it and persuaded the lady likewise to conceal it, which she did, and the matter remained a secret.' (Edited by Andrew Scoble, 1900).

MR RUSSELL: But you see Miss Sutton, this is the point. As I understand it, what is being said, on the defendant's behalf is this: there *was* a pre-contract, it *did* bastardise the Princes, therefore Richard had a true claim to the throne and therefore he had no need to kill them. That's what I understand the suggestion to be.

MISS SUTTON: Exactly.

MR RUSSELL: But the fact of the matter is whether or not that was a valid pre-contract, he had every reason to have them disposed of because parliament at any time could have reversed that illegitimacy. As Henry VII did two years later when he came to the throne.

MISS SUTTON: I don't agree.

MR RUSSELL: But why don't you agree? Parliament could have, and did.

MISS SUTTON: Not while Richard was on the throne and in, in control of the Princes.

MR RUSSELL: But could have. He was not safe with the Princes in the Tower just because they had been bastardised in the manner which we have heard described.

MISS SUTTON: The pre-contract and their illegitimacy remains true. Whether parliament speaks or not.

MR RUSSELL: Providing it has been properly proved and, and certainly if the uprising in October, the autumn rebellion, was upon the basis as it is suggested in the *Chronicles*, firstly upon the basis of freeing the Princes it clearly didn't seem to have very much effect on all those nobles of the south and Wales who supported that rebellion. They didn't seem to worry.

MR DILLON: With great respect, I don't agree with the factual basis upon which Mr Russell has made that suggestion. I'm sorry to intervene but I cannot accept the factual basis that it's suggested in the *Chronicles* that the uprising in Wales and the south and so on was to free the Princes. In fact the uprising was to put Henry VII on the throne and that could only have been done if the Princes of course were dead.

MR RUSSELL: Well I'm sorry but Mr Dillon is not right about that. May I quote from the *Croyland Chronicle*. Miss Sutton, I don't know whether you are aware of this or not; what is said in the *Croyland Chronicle* is this: 'in the meantime and while these things were going on, the two sons of King Edward before named, remained in the Tower of London in the custody of certain persons appointed for that purpose. In order to deliver them from this captivity the people of the southern and western parts of the kingdom began to murmur greatly and to form meetings and confederacies.' That led to the autumn rebellion.

MISS SUTTON: I think it goes on to say that they then thought that they'd rescue the girls.

MR RUSSELL: Then, then what it goes on to say Miss Sutton – you may be right about that, I haven't got the whole report in front of me – yes, I beg your pardon, I have. Then goes on to say, to free the girls, and then goes on to say that then the rumour was spread that the Princes were dead and it was at that stage that the rebellion turned to Henry Tudor. Those are the facts aren't they. And what I'm suggesting to you is that if, if that be right, that the rebellion started upon the basis of freeing the Princes, well then all those nobles of the south and it was the whole of the south of England virtually, wasn't it.

MISS SUTTON: That's a slight exaggeration.

MR RUSSELL: Maybe it is. A lot of the south of England and Wales supported that rebellion to free the Princes, whether or not they were bastards.

MISS SUTTON: There were a lot of people involved in that rebellion who had their own personal axes to grind.

MR RUSSELL: Yes, thank you very much.

MR DILLON: I'm so sorry, I don't wish to quibble on small matters but this may be important. You see the *Chronicle* goes on after referring to the design to free some of the King's daughters: 'At last' – and this is half way down the page and in the next paragraph – 'it was determined by the people in the vicinity of the city of London and certain other counties' –

JUDGE: What page is that?

MR DILLON: 491. Just half way down.

JUDGE: 'At last it was determined . . .'

MR DILLON: Yes – 'as well as some others of the southern counties of the kingdom, to avenge their grievances before stated.' Which was in fact, if one reads the whole document, in my submission, the seizure of the wealth of King Edward IV by Richard III. Then it goes on: 'A proclamation was made that Henry Duke of Buckingham, had repented of his former conduct and would be the chief mover in this attempt, while a rumour was spread that the sons of King Edward IV had died a violent death but it was uncertain how.' Thank you very much Miss Sutton.

Then Mr Potter. My Lord this is my last witness.

Mr Jeremy Potter

MR DILLON: Mr Potter, it's Ronald Jeremy Potter. I think you're the chairman of a publishing group in London and chairman of the Richard III Society and have been since 1971. Published a number of works, included amongst which, published by a house other than your own, is the book I hold in my hand from which my friend has in fact already quoted, *Good King Richard?* now then can I ask you one or two short questions please. Firstly, it's become clear during the time evidence has been given that some of the items on which historians now fasten, have come to light only very recently: Mancini for instance in 1934; the College of Arms fragment in only 1980. Is research in this field and upon the question which is posed for the jury here complete yet?

MR POTTER: No, there are developments going on the whole time, that's perfectly true. In the 1930s Mancini was found and the bones were examined. In the 1970s there were two important new discoveries in connection with the National Portrait Gallery exhibition. And as you say, only in 1980 this fragment of chronicle was discovered at the College of Arms. There could well be documents in archives in this country, abroad, in places like Burgundy, Brussels, where the Burgundian archives are, the Vatican and so on, yes.

JUDGE: A pretty sparse period for the keeping of records in any event, wasn't it.

MR POTTER: A surprising number have survived, my Lord, actually, yes.

MR DILLON: Well now can I turn to Richard straight away please. I asked Mr Richards about his character up to the death of Edward IV. What, how would you put it?

MR POTTER: Well I would put it that at the time when Edward IV died, Richard was a man of excellent character. He'd remained unswervingly loyal to his brother, unlike Clarence or Warwick during the long wars against Lancaster. He was the leader of the vanguard at the battles of Barnet and Tewkesbury. He was a courageous man. He'd spent eleven years as his brother's viceroy, governing the north of England where he had a reputation for just and fair administration. In fact, Mancini himself who we've heard, is no, was no Richard lover, said 'the good reputation of his private life and his public activities powerfully attracted the esteem of strangers'. And he was thirty at this time. His record was unblemished, he was loyal, he was brave, he was pious, he was just, and he was the last man that anyone would have expected to have killed Edward IV's sons.

MR DILLON: He had taken them into his care, in effect, during the time in London. Would that have had an effect upon Richard and his view of them?

MR POTTER: After Edward IV died?

MR DILLON: Yes.

MR POTTER: He behaved impeccably of course, and the boys came under his protection. As has been stated, he led an act of public fealty in York. He did the same thing when he arrived in London. He led the Lords, he led the City fathers in acts of fealty to his nephew and throughout May, for five weeks, every act, everything that was done in the country was in the name of Edward V.

MR DILLON: The late King Edward IV expressly put the children in the protection of Richard, did he not?

MR POTTER: The realm certainly, and with it the children.

MR DILLON: So he had the particular responsibility in respect of them.

MR POTTER: Yes.

MR DILLON: And did, in your view, discharge that obligation upon him.

MR POTTER: I think he behaved impeccably. The reason why he has a bad reputation is that the Tudors had to say that he was being hypocritical and deceitful. If he'd behaved badly, they'd have said, look how badly he behaved. Since he behaved very well, they said he must be a hypocrite.

MR DILLON: So his outward display didn't mirror his actual performance.

MR POTTER: There is no reason to suppose that his motives were impure.

MR DILLON: He had real reason, it's quite clear from the evidence which has been given already, to fear the south, was unpractised in the court, hardly came to London, in the decade or so preceding 1483.

MR POTTER: Yes I think it should be understood that the split between north and south at the end of the fifteenth century was somewhat similar, in fact rather greater, than it is today. And people in the north were much poorer. They were regarded by the south as dangerous savages and the real peculiarity of Richard III is that he is the only king of England who has come from the north, with northern support, his northern affinity, to claim the throne. And this naturally upset southerners, men of Edward's household, Edward IV's household, who lost their jobs to these intruding northerners, savages from places like Yorkshire.

MR DILLON: Well, the real reason to fear a plot against him from the Woodvilles, who don't sound a very attractive lot.

MR POTTER: Well the Woodvilles made a pre-emptive strike for power as I think is agreed. And this naturally put Richard on his mettle. And then it became clear in my view that the sensible thing was that Richard should become king. I mean a boy king would have been a disaster. Nobody wanted a boy king. It would have started the civil war over again. The point about Richard's assumption was that his coronation was one of the best attended in history. Everyone actually, except the rival power groups, recognised that it was the sensible and logical thing. If Richard remained as protector, he was open in two or three years time to the vengeance of the Woodvilles. And not only Richard himself, but everyone who had supported him, all his affinity.

MR DILLON: How much importance then do you attach to the evidence given, if that's the right way to describe it, by Bishop Stillington about the pre-contract?

MR POTTER: Well I think Stillington was probably right. Stillington was a man of considerable importance. He'd been Chancellor of England for seven years under Edward IV, which was the number one job in the country, equivalent to the prime minister today. And so Stillington was very far from being a nobody. Certainly his evidence at this time was very convenient.

JUDGE: He was Lord Chancellor at the time?

MR POTTER: He was Chancellor under Edward IV, not at the time. He had fallen out with Edward IV and been imprisoned at the time of Clarence's disgrace. And some historians assume that the reason for his disgrace was that Stillington told Clarence some years earlier of this pre-contract which would have made Clarence the heir to the throne and not the boys and that was the reason for Clarence's execution.

MR DILLON: Clarence, just remind us, is the gentleman who is said to have died in a 'butt of malmsey' I think.

MR POTTER: Yes. Clarence was the brother who stood between Edward IV and Richard, and if he had been alive would have had a better claim than Richard's. And perhaps I should also make this point, that he had a son alive who was called Edward Earl of Warwick and this was another nephew of Richard's and his claim to the throne was better than Richard's, except that he was disbarred by Clarence's attainder. And this was a nephew of Richard's in precisely the same position as the Princes. Attainders were readily reversible. Parliament could have reversed Edward of Warwick's attainder and that would have given him a better claim to the throne than Richard.

And what happened to Edward of Warwick? We happen to know. He was well treated by Richard, he was kept up in Yorkshire in a royal nursery with Edward IV's daughters. And he was even made Richard's heir at one time. He survived Richard's reign quite happily and of course immediately after Bosworth, he was put in the Tower of London by Henry Tudor and judicially murdered some years later. So we do know what happened to one nephew who had a very good claim to the throne – as good as the two Princes once they'd been declared illegitimate.

Well then, what do you say about the pressure, inevitable pressure as the prosecution like to describe it, upon Richard to kill the Princes because if they stayed alive, those nephews, they were a threat to Richard?

MR POTTER: I don't see that their death was necessary to him at all. They were in a quite different position from the other deposed monarchs, Edward II, Richard II and Henry VI. Those were crowned and annointed kings. Edward V was proclaimed but he was never crowned and annointed and it was the annointing that gave a medieval king semi-divine status. Which was why it was high treason, a mortal sin, to kill him. He was the Lord's annointed. Edward V was not the Lord's annointed and he'd been declared illegitimate. Of course they were some kind of a threat to him. But when he was the crowned and annointed king he was home and dry, on 6th July 1483, when everybody accepts that the boys were still alive.

You see in the overseas chronicles, the French, there is the assumption that he had to kill the boys in order to become king, but he didn't. He became king while the boys were still alive. Once he was king, they were less of a threat to him than Buckingham and Henry Tudor, and Henry Tudor and Buckingham's claim to the throne was very much worse than the two boys. And it was in Richard's interest, in my view, to keep the boys alive. They were much more of an embarrassment to Henry Tudor and to Buckingham if Buckingham was aiming to the throne. And it's hypocritical of Henry Tudor to shed tears over the boys. If Henry Tudor had beaten Richard he would have had to have killed the boys, otherwise he would not have been accepted as king.

MR DILLON: Because they stood in his way.

MR POTTER: Yes.

MR DILLON: But the same is true of Buckingham, so let us concentrate for a moment if we may upon Buckingham. He had a good and direct title as we can see from the little chart that the jury have already got. We know that he'd got his eyes on the crown because the chroniclers tell us and that's been agreed in cross-examination. Can I follow the chronology immediately after the coronation please. Because Richard and the Queen left London first, leaving Buckingham behind. Am I right in thinking that it wasn't until Richard and the Queen reached Gloucester, where they were between the 29th July and the 2nd August, that Buckingham joined them there, stayed for a short time and then went straight on to Brecon, to his estates in Wales? That's the order of events I think.

MR POTTER: Yes.

MR DILLON: At Brecon at that time was Bishop Morton detained. That is the man who later became Archbishop of England and in whose household More was brought up. The chroniclers describe Buckingham and Morton's conversation and indeed it's right to say, even in the old fashioned edition that I've got of More, the More history of Richard breaks off during their conversation, which began soon after – according to More who might have known about this fact at any rate – soon after Buckingham arrived there.

MR POTTER: Yes. I mean may I say something about Buckingham not being with Richard on the royal progress? Buckingham had the opportunity at that point to kill the Princes. He was the Constable of England.* Brackenbury who was the Lieutenant of the Tower could not have denied him entry. There were many stories going on for many years about what had happened to the Princes, and Buckingham is mentioned in four or five chronicles as a possible murderer.† Now I wouldn't want to accuse Buckingham of the murder any more than I want anyone to accuse Richard of it. It was certainly a highly plausible thing. There were other stories about what happened to the

---

* Buckingham was Constable of England, a job analogous to the modern Chief of the General Staff. One of the specific responsibilities of the Constable was to oversee the running of military buildings and fortifications. The Tower of London, being the chief military stronghold of the capital as well as a royal residence, was under his jurisdiction. Buckingham theoretically had the right to go to the Tower and demand entry of his subordinate, the Lieutenant of the Tower, Sir Robert Brackenbury.

† The sources are: A fragment of narrative, the MS Ashmole 1448–60 of uncertain date and origin, *Historical Notes of a London Citizen 1483–88*, *The Memoires* of Philippe de Commynes and the *Chronicles* of Jean Molinet.

Princes, that they were smuggled abroad, which is even said by Polydore Vergil, they were going on for years. Of course there were rumours that the boys had been killed at the Tower. But Henry Tudor when he became king was just as much plagued by rumours that the boys were alive as Richard had been plagued by rumours that they were dead.

MR DILLON: He had to face Lambert Simnell.

MR POTTER: Lambert Simnell, Perkin Warbeck.* Perkin Warbeck was accepted as the younger Prince by most of the states of Europe. The king of Scotland gave him his cousin to marry.

MR DILLON: Well then, can I come back to the conversation between Buckingham and Morton, because Buckingham is virtually speaking hot foot from London. Was the conversation between those two as reported by the chronicles 'Let us start an uprising to free the Princes', or was it 'Let us start an uprising to put Henry Tudor on the throne'?

MR POTTER: Well the idea that Buckingham wanted to see Henry Tudor on the throne is, I think, a total illusion. Buckingham was going for the throne himself. Of course he would have said that he was supporting Henry Tudor if it helped to topple Richard. But once he got Henry Tudor over from Brittany, Buckingham's power in England was probably stronger than Henry Tudor's and there's no doubt in my mind that Buckingham was aiming for the throne. Buckingham had been the number one man to Richard and it was said that he became jealous the moment Richard was crowned. And he thought that he would do better I think to ally himself with Henry Tudor and with the Woodvilles and get Richard off the throne.

JUDGE: It would have been a tremendous step for Buckingham to take, would it not, Richard still being alive, just been crowned, for him suddenly, apparently without the knowledge of King Richard according to your theory, to have killed the Princes.

---

* Lambert Simnel was probably born in 1475, the son of an Oxford man. He first pretended to be Richard Duke of York, the younger of the two princes. Later he adopted the title of Earl of Warwick, the son of George Duke of Clarence, the executed brother of Edward IV and Richard. When captured by Henry VII he was sent to work as a scullion and later rose to be falconer. He died in 1525. Perkin Warbeck was probably born about 1474. First he assumed the role of the Earl of Warwick, then later, with the support of Margaret of Burgundy, the sister of Edward IV and Richard III, was hailed as Richard of York. He was captured and imprisoned by Henry VII in 1497 and executed two years later.

MR POTTER: Buckingham was the impressario, the stage manager of Richard's accession to the throne.

JUDGE: That may be.

MR POTTER: And he probably saw himself as a Warwick the King Maker, and Warwick the King Maker of course changed sides when the particular king didn't suit him.*

MR DILLON: Really, the conversation according to More began so soon after Buckingham arrived and joined Morton; Henry did in fact land, but abortively. Buckingham did in fact rise but was caught and was executed at Salisbury. So can I come on to the events subsequently because in February/March 1484 the Queen released the daughters, including Elizabeth, whom Henry Tudor had undertaken to marry by then, into the power of Richard. What's your view about that?

MR POTTER: Well if the Woodvilles thought that Richard had killed the boys their behaviour really becomes quite inexplicable. Not only does Elizabeth Woodville, the boys' mother, release all the girls into Richard's power, she sends for her son, Dorset – her son by a previous marriage – to come home, to leave Henry Tudor and come and join Richard. And then later on of course she and Elizabeth of York, her daughter, plan a marriage with Richard and there is a surviving reference to a letter from Elizabeth of York, the boys' sister, saying that she is 'Richard's in heart, and in body, and in soul'. And the idea that she would have written those sort of things about someone who had murdered her brothers is, I think, unthinkable.†

MR DILLON: Well I'm going to ask about five other very short matters. Once Henry VII had defeated Richard at Bosworth and assumed the throne himself, is there any evidence that he made any kind of enquiry about the Princes' death?

MR POTTER: Henry?

MR DILLON: Yes.

MR POTTER: I mean one of the extraordinary things to me is that there is no direct contemporary accusation of Richard as the murderer of the Princes. There is this peculiar reference in a poem by some doggerel

* Richard Neville, Earl of Warwick, the most powerful magnate in England, helped Edward IV take the throne from Henry VI. He later quarrelled with Edward, possibly about foreign policy, possibly as a result of the Woodvilles' growing influence. He rebelled, and was defeated and killed at the Battle of Barnet in 1471.

† The only reference to this letter is by Sir George Buck in his *History of King Richard III* (ed. A.N. Kincaid, 1979). Buck claimed to have seen the letter from Elizabeth to John Howard, Duke of Norfolk, dated February 1485 in the collection of the Earl of Arundel.

poet which the Croyland chronicler puts in and it is, as we have said, extremely oblique, and it is specifically introduced, as you've mentioned, with the phrases that 'Bosworth avenged the cause of the Princes', not the death . . .

MR DILLON: That's the one that I've asked about.

MR POTTER: Not the death, not the death.

MR DILLON: As one would expect.

MR POTTER: The cause of the Princes. And Mancini, although of course he says that the people are frightened for the fate of the boys and what is going to happen, which is perfectly natural, he specifically says not only that he doesn't know how they were killed, but he didn't even know whether they were killed. Now Henry Tudor's act of attainder against Richard III – when he became king as Henry VII – mentions the phrase 'the shedding of infants blood'; which obviously refers to the Princes. But it is a general accusation and what Henry Tudor needed at that moment was two little bodies and a requiem mass and bury the Princes, bury any thought of pretenders. He never produced them. He never produced a story of what had happened to the Princes to back up this. It took him seventeen years for a framed confession by Tyrell who had remained as captain of one of the Castle's guard in Calais for seventeen years serving Henry Tudor. He was lured onto a battleship in Calais harbour under a promise of a safe conduct. He was put in the Tower and he was executed for treason, conspiring with the current Yorkist pretender, the Earl of Suffolk.

MR DILLON: Now I'm going to stop you, if I may please. Is there any record to be found of that confession anywhere?

MR POTTER: There is no record at all. It was not publicised by Henry Tudor. We only know of it from More. It was despised by Henry Tudor's official historian, Polydore Vergil.

MR DILLON: Well then I'm going to deal with the rest of the matters very shortly. One of the matters that Mr Russell referred to in opening was Richard's silence; that he never produced the bodies, never produced the children, never denied or made any statement about them himself. What do you say about that?

MR POTTER: Well there could have been a number of reasons for that. One of them might have been that he despised the rumours, that it was beneath him to take any notice of them. Another might have been that he thought he could confuse his enemies more if they didn't know whether the boys were alive or dead; and in particular he wouldn't wish to display them so the people wouldn't know their whereabouts. If Buckingham had killed the Princes, of course, he didn't have them to display.

MR DILLON: Would his, given his role and his protection of them, would any denial that he made have been acceptable?

MR POTTER: No. His enemies of course wouldn't have believed him, and I think even deeper than that, if Buckingham had killed them while they were under Richard's protection, he would have felt extremely guilty. I mean he would have felt responsible for their deaths. They were under his protection and someone had killed them.

MR DILLON: Thank you very much indeed.

MR RUSSELL: Mr Potter, I think we can agree probably on the first matter I'm going to put to you. The Woodvilles set about 'a pre-emptive strike for power'. Those I think are your words. That resulted in Richard being summoned by Hastings from the north.

MR POTTER: Yes.

MR RUSSELL: Result of that: Rivers and Grey, two of the leaders of the Woodville faction with the Prince at Stony Stratford, arrested, subsequently to be executed, almost certainly without trial.

MR POTTER: I wouldn't agree with that, actually. There is . . .

MR RUSSELL: I use my words carefully, almost certainly without trial.

MR POTTER: Quite possibly with a trial but under the . . . presided over by the Earl of Northumberland as stated in one of the chronicles.

MR RUSSELL: But very much a barrack room trial, over a very short space of time if it took place at all. Yes?

JUDGE: Killing without trial was not an unusual event in these days, I gather.

MR POTTER: No, it became commoner when the Tudors were on the throne.

JUDGE: That's a good *tu quoque* if I may say so.

MR RUSSELL: It was also against the desire of the council, the royal council, wasn't it? Who had specifically refused to ratify their execution.

MR POTTER: Well, what happened was . . .

MR RUSSELL: Well that's right isn't it? Firstly.

MR POTTER: They, yes, would – may I state the grounds on this?

MR RUSSELL: No Mr Potter. First of all please just answer the question. That is correct isn't it.

MR POTTER: Initially yes.

MR RUSSELL: Oh yes initially, thereafter Richard ordered their execution without further reference to the council.

MR POTTER: Did he?

MR RUSSELL: I'm suggesting to you that's what happened.

MR POTTER: Oh, I'm suggesting that is quite wrong. I'm suggesting that the council, the later council did authorise their execution. There's no reason to suppose that Richard ordered it himself.

MR RUSSELL: Is there any evidence of that?

MR POTTER: There's no evidence that he acted individually.

MR RUSSELL: Is there any evidence that the council authorised it?

MR POTTER: There is no evidence that they didn't.

MR RUSSELL: Is there any evidence that they did?

MR POTTER: No.

MR RUSSELL: Thank you.

MR POTTER: But there wouldn't be.

MR RUSSELL: The result was that, the result that followed from that was that Richard clearly then set about the crown.

MR POTTER: I don't think those two facts are connected, no.

MR RUSSELL: Richard set about for the crown at some stage, did he not?

MR POTTER: Yes.

MR RUSSELL: And do you accept, which is again suggested directly by the chroniclers, that Hastings having had his views on that asked for by Buckingham, made it absolutely clear that he would have no truck with that suggestion?

MR POTTER: I would suggest Richard aimed for the crown as a result of Bucking, er Hastings' conspiracy to kill him.

MR RUSSELL: Now why should Hastings possibly wish to conspire to kill Richard when Hastings was accepting and summoning Richard to protect his, Richard's, protectorship?

MR POTTER: Because Buckingham, as you've just mentioned, I think, and it is mentioned in the chronicles, sounded Hastings out as to whether he would accept Richard as king.

MR RUSSELL: Precisely. And Hastings said no.

MR POTTER: Yes.

MR RUSSELL: And the result of that was that Hastings was dealt with by way of trick arrest and immediate execution.

MR POTTER: Hastings was plotting against Richard's life.

MR RUSSELL: There is no evidence of any sort to support that proposition, is there.

MR POTTER: Can I mention three pieces of evidence?

MR RUSSELL: Yes please.

MR POTTER: The first of all, the letter that Richard wrote to York, that there was a plot against his life; secondly, . . .

MR RUSSELL: By the Woodvilles.

MR POTTER: Hastings had allied himself to the Woodvilles.

MR RUSSELL: Hastings was totally anti-Woodville, Mr Potter.

MR POTTER: No, I'm sorry, Hastings . . .

MR RUSSELL: Well do you agree with the evidence of Mr Richards about . . .

MR POTTER: No I don't. The whole point was that Hastings swung back to the Woodvilles because his nose had been put out of joint by Buckingham.

MR RUSSELL: Where's the evidence of that?

MR POTTER: Hastings, that is in the situation.

MR RUSSELL: In the what?

MR POTTER: In the situation.

MR RUSSELL: No. Where is the evidence that Hastings swung back to the Woodvilles.

MR POTTER: We are both speculating, are we not?

MR RUSSELL: Well I'm not speculating. Because I at least have the backing of Mancini. Mancini . . .

MR POTTER: Can, can I say something about Mancini?

MR RUSSELL: Well in a minute, Mr Potter, but perhaps we ought to move on a little. The fact of the matter is that Hastings was dealt with in a way which shocked, horrified and appalled and still does.

MR POTTER: As a result of a plot, and that College of Arms document clearly states that there was a Hastings plot and that dates from the 1480s, it's much earlier.

MR RUSSELL: Prince Richard was got out of sanctuary by a trick and lies. Correct?

MR POTTER: No I wouldn't say that at all.

MR RUSSELL: Prince Richard was got out of sanctuary on the pretext that he was required for his brother's coronation?

MR POTTER: According to whom?

MR RUSSELL: According to Mancini.

MR POTTER: Yes, well I wouldn't trust Mancini on that point.

MR RUSSELL: Why not?

MR POTTER: Well, Mancini's sources were Edwardian loyalists; Mancini did not speak English in the view of his editor. He had a very limited view, he was an honest reporter as I have said, but he had a very limited view. He never got involved on Richard's side. He doesn't seem to have spoken to anyone putting that point of view. He was against Richard, he was against the Woodvilles. His information came from people who thought the same way as Hastings, so he would naturally say that Hastings' plot was an invention of Richards. That would be quite natural, but we don't have to believe him.

MR RUSSELL: No, but the trouble is Mr Potter that whenever the chroniclers, such as Mancini and Croyland, say something detrimental to Richard then the pro-Ricardians then say 'unreliable', don't they?

MR POTTER: Well that's a statement with which I don't agree and if it is played, it is played the other way just as much.

MR RUSSELL: Why would you think the Princes' mother was persuaded to allow the Prince to be taken out of the safe sanctuary of the Abbey?

MR POTTER: Because she trusted Richard, I would say. You see the Tower was the right place for the boy to be. It was a royal palace, his brother presumably wanted company, and that was the right place for him to be.

MR RUSSELL: It was the wrong place for him to be because he didn't stay there for very long, did he. He ended up under the staircase, Mr Potter.

MR POTTER: Well, according to you; I'm doubtful about those bones, I'm sorry to have to say, I mean, the sex, the century is not known.

MR RUSSELL: Mr Potter, again, this is the trouble. The Ricardians had a good run until the early 1930s and then Mancini was discovered in the library at Lille; his record. And then the bones were discovered the following year. And both of them were a bitter blow to those who had been supporting Richard, weren't they?

MR POTTER: No. The bones don't prove, even if the bones were genuine, they don't prove that Richard killed the boys.

MR RUSSELL: No, but they prove that they were killed in the Tower.

MR POTTER: If they are true, they do. It is likely that they were killed in the Tower. But it is not certain.

MR RUSSELL: And there is no way, is there Mr Potter, that they could have been killed in the Tower by anyone without Richard at least knowing about it?

MR POTTER: He would have known about it afterwards, but not necessarily at the time, and can I point out that if you are going to kill people in the Tower and get rid of their bodies, you do not bury them very deeply in the ground. There is an easily available exit which is the Water Gate.

MR RUSSELL: They weren't discovered for two hundred years and then only by mistake?

MR POTTER: Other bodies were discovered and decided that they were the Princes. There were bodies discovered in 1647 as well as 1674.

MR RUSSELL: If you accept, Mr Potter, if you accept as I think you did a moment or two ago, that if someone had killed the Princes in the Tower then Richard must have known, well then he remained silent did he not?

MR POTTER: That is true.

MR RUSSELL: For the whole of the rest of his life. Not for very long, for two years or so.

MR POTTER: That is true.

MR RUSSELL: He never sought to find out who had killed them, and accuse that person.

MR POTTER: He – if it was Buckingham . . .

MR RUSSELL: No, don't let's worry about Buckingham for the moment. Anybody, whoever had killed those Princes – and I suggest no one could possibly have got into the Tower with Brackenbury, the keeper, holding the keys and kill those Princes without Richard knowing, within the time it took a horse rider to get from London to wherever Richard was.

MR POTTER: A Constable of England could certainly have got in, in the King's absence.

MR RUSSELL: Not without Brackenbury the keeper knowing.

MR POTTER: No, you're quite right.

MR RUSSELL: Right.

MR POTTER: But that does not mean that Richard knew at the time. It means that he would have known afterwards.

MR RUSSELL: Within a few – within a few days.

MR POTTER: Yes, of course.

MR RUSSELL: Oh of course, I'd accept that.

JUDGE: Brackenbury was a friend and an ally of the king was he not?

MR POTTER: Exactly, he would have told the king instantly.

MR RUSSELL: There could be no possible reason for Richard, with the rumours that were flying around and his insecure position on the throne, there was no possible reason for him to remain silent or not enquire from Brackenbury as to who had done this dreadful deed. And accuse. . . .

MR POTTER: If he knew that somebody had done it he could well have chosen to keep quiet. Because as I said earlier, his enemies would have blamed him, he may have felt guilty himself, he may have wished to keep his enemies guessing as to whether the boys were still alive, it was important that Henry Tudor shouldn't know whether they were alive or dead. There are plenty of reasons why he wouldn't have said anything.

MR RUSSELL: In reality the only possible reason for him keeping quiet was because he knew perfectly well that it could only be to his detriment because he must have been a party to it.

MR POTTER: No, I don't think so.

JUDGE: Can I just ask one further question on the bones?

MR RUSSELL: M'Lord, please.

JUDGE: It would have been a very remarkable coincidence if it happened that two other children, of about this age, were both found in a box, in, in non-consecrated ground, in the Tower. But you say 'no they weren't the Princes'.

MR POTTER: My Lord . . .

JUDGE: It's a very strange coincidence.

MR POTTER: There were two other bodies discovered, some thirty years earlier.

JUDGE: Of children.

MR POTTER: Of children. There was another one which was subsequently discovered to be one of the Tower apes. But the date, the dates of the bodies are not known. They could be Roman, the skeletons I mean. We're going through hundreds of years, possibly. All that we know is that the bones are pre-1647 and the Tower was a well-inhabited building throughout the Middle Ages.

MR RUSSELL: Mr Potter, of course you have to say that, don't you? You cannot accept that those bones are almost certainly, I don't put it any higher than that, almost certainly the bones of the Princes because it blows a lot of the Ricardian argument sky high, doesn't it?

MR POTTER: No, it doesn't. No, it doesn't.

MR RUSSELL: Let me ask you about one or two questions. . . .

MR POTTER: It only blows sky high those who thought that Henry Tudor had done it, which is a position that I have never occupied and which, as far as I know, very few people suggest now.

MR RUSSELL: No, I think that's right.

MR POTTER: I mean, that was the whole point about it. It was said that it had altered the date, so they had to have been killed in '83, and Henry killed them.

MR RUSSELL: Now I must leave that topic, Mr Potter, because I have to ask you about two other things. I want to ask you a question about Buckingham and then about the release of the daughters from the sanctuary. Let's assume for the purposes of these questions that Buckingham did in fact, or was a major party to the killing of the Princes. Because if Richard is responsible, Buckingham almost certainly was. Would you agree with that?

MR POTTER: Well, I'm deeply suspicious of Buckingham, I would say that.

MR RUSSELL: Well now, let's assume that he had a motive of his own. Perhaps he saw getting rid of them as a way to the crown for himself in due course.

MR POTTER: And also blackening Richard's name, yes.

MR RUSSELL: Yes, but that's a very weak argument, isn't it Mr Potter?

MR POTTER: No, I don't think it is at all.

MR RUSSELL: I mean, you're not seriously suggesting that Buckingham would go into the Tower and murder those two boys in order to be able to let it be mooted abroad that Richard might have done it and so blacken his name? You're not really suggesting that?

MR POTTER: Plus, clearing his own way to the throne. The double . . .

MR RUSSELL: As His Lordship was saying to you, it's almost inconceivable, isn't it? It would have been a tremendous step for Buckingham to take, to have done this, if I may use the expression, off his own bat.

MR POTTER: Buckingham was a very unstable character, as I think is generally agreed.

MR RUSSELL: Is there any evidence at all, anywhere, from anybody, to suggest that Buckingham had done that murder on his own?

MR POTTER: Well it depends how you read some of the chronicles. I mean, the College of Arms one says that the boys were killed 'on the vise' and you can either say that's 'on the advice' or you can say it's 'by the device of'.

MR RUSSELL: But that's not evidence that he did it on his own.

MR POTTER: If you read it as 'device', which is just as good and Richard is not mentioned, it is a possible indication that Buckingham did it on his own.

MR RUSSELL: Yes. Well now, you have been saying that Buckingham had lots of opportunity because he stayed in London after the coronation. Any evidence to support that?

MR POTTER: Yes. The King went to Oxford . . .

MR RUSSELL: For a dinner at Magdalen College and Buckingham wasn't on the guest list. That was ten days, ten days or so after the coronation?

I forget the precise date. But it doesn't mean to say Buckingham was in London, does it?

MR POTTER: No. But I think it is said that Buckingham joined Richard at Gloucester from London.

MR RUSSELL: On the 20 . . .? No.

MR POTTER: Because he went on to Brecon.

MR RUSSELL: No, with respect, not from London. He next turns up in Gloucester, I think on 29th July, and goes on to Brecon.

MR POTTER: Well, let's accept that.

MR RUSSELL: The only evidence about Buckingham is that between the 6th July and 29th July nobody knows where he was, except that he was not at Oxford with the King to have dinner at Magdalen College about ten days . . . about 16th July. That's all we know. So there's absolutely no evidence that he stayed behind in London and, indeed, he might have been on the Royal progress and just not attended the dinner for some reason.

MR POTTER: Well, it may be, yes.

MR RUSSELL: All I want to establish is, a lot of your questions in answer to my learned friend have been upon the basis that Buckingham stayed behind in London and all I'm suggesting to you is that there's not a shred of evidence to support that.

MR POTTER: Well, there isn't a shred of evidence that Richard killed the Princes.

MR RUSSELL: No, that's not what I'm asking you.

MR POTTER: We're speculating.

MR RUSSELL: No, we're not speculating. All I'm establishing from you is that there is no evidence whatsoever that Buckingham stayed behind in London.

MR POTTER: No. It is a presumption that if he wasn't at Oxford, that he wasn't on the Royal Progress and that he would have stayed in London. It is a presumption for which there is no evidence.

MR RUSSELL: And if Buckingham had done it, there was absolutely no reason for Richard not to accuse him, at least at the time of his execution for treason after the rebellion in October.

MR POTTER: Well, I think there is and I've stated those reasons before. It is very significant that after the meeting at Gloucester, it was then that Buckingham went off to Brecon and joined the other side and my interpretation of that is that the quarrel between Buckingham and Richard was over the murder of the Princes. They never met again. Richard called him 'the most untrue creature living' and refused to meet him before his execution at Salisbury.

MR RUSSELL: And that was the moment and the opportunity for him to say 'Buckingham you are a murderer. Arrest him, try him and execute him' before he had a chance to join the rebellion which was then mounting itself.

MR POTTER: Buckingham was far too powerful to be arrested immediately at short notice.

MR RUSSELL: Hastings, Hastings had been disposed of within half an hour.

MR POTTER: Hastings was in London where Richard had the power. Gloucester was in the West Country where Buckingham had his power base.

MR RUSSELL: Then finally, Mr Potter, the daughters. The daughters had been in sanctuary for some time, I think since June, no April I suppose it was that they went into sanctuary, and they were finally released early in the following year. Correct? I'm seeking your confirmation of that.

MR POTTER: I think March '84, something like that.

MR RUSSELL: I'm grateful. I thought it was January but it's March apparently. But by that time Richard was fairly firmly on the throne, was he not?

MR POTTER: Yes.

MR RUSSELL: I mean, he'd taken the throne, he'd subdued the rebellion in October and was there, fairly solidly. Elizabeth, how shall we describe her? She was a pretty tough lady, wasn't she? Not a very popular lady. She was in this position wasn't she? There she was with her five daughters, been in Westminster Abbey, in the sanctuary there, I think in the Abbot's house for nine months or so, or getting on for a year. Sanctuary wasn't all that safe, in any event, was it? I mean, they could have been removed at any time.*

MR POTTER: Yes, I mean, it was unlikely but . . .

MR RUSSELL: There were precedents for that. I mean, sanctuary had been broken by force on other occasions.

MR POTTER: Not, I think, where women were involved. It was the Tudors that killed women but not the Plantagenets.

---

* In 1454, Richard Duke of York, father of Richard III, had seized the Duke of Exeter in sanctuary in Westminster Abbey. In 1471, Edward IV had forced the sanctuary at Tewkesbury Abbey to capture Edward Beaufort, Duke of Somerset and other Lancastrians.

MR RUSSELL: There was little prospect at that time of any challenge to Richard, was there not?

MR POTTER: No.

MR RUSSELL: She was really faced with this situation. She either stayed there and let her daughters grow up for another year or two in sanctuary, or she accepted the offer which was made by Richard, and the offer was a fairly handsome one, wasn't it? He gave many pledges as to what he would do with the daughters as to their safety and marrying them off and so on.

MR POTTER: Yes.

MR RUSSELL: So she had Richard's assurance, she really had no alternative but to let those girls out and Richard didn't really care about the women in the family, did he?

MR POTTER: Henry Tudor had said that he would marry Elizabeth of York. He'd sworn on the high altar at Rennes Cathedral the previous Christmas, he had got the support of the dissident Yorkists by saying that; she was most important to Richard.

MR RUSSELL: Now that is the point, is it not? That autumn rebellion, which, maybe it started to free the Princes, maybe it started in some other way, but ended up with Yorkists changing camp and supporting a Tudor claimant, a Lancastrian claimant to the throne in the person of Henry Tudor.

MR POTTER: These were southerners who had been deprived of their estates by Richard's northerners. This was a north/south argument.

MR RUSSELL: They were southerners and they were pro-Edward IV and Edward V loyalists to a man.

MR POTTER: Well you say 'to a man'. I mean, there were a handful of them. Most people didn't leave the south of England for Brittany.

MR RUSSELL: But the rebellion went through, what, seven counties?

MR POTTER: A very small number of people involved, easily put down.

MR RUSSELL: Well, it was easily put down because there were very few troops in fact around them and Henry Tudor, on his way over the Channel, hit a storm and the two thousand men he was bringing over never got there.

MR POTTER: A very small number of people in the south of England, it was widespread and . . .

MR RUSSELL: The reason why Yorkists espoused their cause and supported a Lancastrian on the throne, or possibly on the throne, in the person of Henry Tudor, was because they were so appalled at Richard's treatment of the Princes.

MR POTTER: The *Croyland Chronicle* specifically says that they were concerned about the plantation of northerners in the south.

MR RUSSELL: Yes, thank you Mr Potter. If His Lordship has any questions . . .

JUDGE: Thank you Mr Potter.

MR DILLON: Thank you Mr Potter, and that is all the evidence that I have to call.

JUDGE: Now do you wish to address the jury?

MR RUSSELL: M'Lord, yes.

JUDGE: For the prosecution, Mr Russell . . .

MR RUSSELL: It'll only take a very few minutes, members of the jury. But the fact is, and you may think, and I suggest that you should, that this has been conclusively proved, is that these young boys were killed and buried secretly in the Tower where they had been incarcerated by their uncle, this defendant, when he seized the throne. And this just could not have happened without Richard knowing about it and condoning it. It's as simple as that and we start upon that very firm and sound basis, particularly where all the evidence supports that interpretation and really nothing detracts from it. Everything Richard did points to his guilt and nothing specifically, other than assumption, points to his innocence. Members of the jury, that is in a sentence, why we suggest that he is probably guilty of this murder. And I use that word 'probably' advisedly because, as His Lordship told you at the commencement of this trial, that is the onus which is upon the prosecution to prove, to satisfy you in the special circumstances in this case, of the guilt of the defendant.

Of course, the evidence is circumstantial and largely hearsay. It has to be. It must be. Where all the witnesses have long since departed this life and, of course members of the jury, I don't know what's going on through your minds, I don't know what points, in the evidence, you may be querying, I don't know which parts of the evidence satisfy you. Let me just try, over the next few minutes, just to summarise that evidence, just to see if I can help you arrive at your proper verdict.

Well, where do we start? We start with the bones. That the anatomist and the historical facts, particularly that the Princes, those two boys, were in the Tower at that time and people had said that they were buried in the place where those bones were found, makes the coincidence too great you may think, certainly on the balance of probabilities, too great not to be those of the Princes, despite what Mr. Potter may still try to persuade you to the contrary. Who had the motive? Well, the answer is primarily, if not solely, Richard. And the events underline that motive: the power of the Woodvilles, the fear of the Woodvilles, which brings Richard hurrying South at Hasting's requirement. And what does he do? He sets about destroying that powerful faction, the Woodvilles. Grey and Rivers arrested and subsequently executed; the Council having refused to condone that act, and there being no evidence, as Mr Potter has just told you, there being no evidence that any subsequent Council agreed to that course of action. The two heirs to the throne are held in the Tower. There's no question, is there, but that Richard, the younger of the two, was removed from sanctuary by deceit and by deception on the pretext, this being 16th June, on the pretext that he was required to attend his brother's Coronation. It is very clear that by this stage, members of the jury you may think, that Richard already was setting out to obtain the crown for himself because, within five days, the question of the bastardisation is being shouted from the pulpit of St Paul's. Hence, as the *Croyland Chronicle* says, the corruption of the preachers.

Members of the jury, it really doesn't matter in one sense at what stage Richard set his own sights on the crown because that decision was taken at some time and for your purposes, you may think, that's really all that matters. Who stood in his way? Hastings. Because Hastings said 'no' when Buckingham attempted to find out whether Hastings would agree. And what happened to Hastings? Well, I needn't repeat it. You have heard. Asked to come to a council which was split, a half meeting in the Tower, he's arrested and executed immediately, without trial. A state of affairs which appalled the populace and the establishment in particular. Well members of the jury, the Princes were still very much in evidence. They were still in the Tower and, obviously they were still a dangerous rallying point, for the faithful Yorkist followers of their father and, so strongly did they feel, that there was this rebellion in October when, as we've just established through Mr Potter, the Yorkists – this was still in the time of the conflict between Lancaster and York – the Yorkists were prepared to espouse that cause and support Henry Tudor, a Lancastrian.

Well members of the jury, what was he going to do about the boys? Well, the first stage was to declare them illegitimate and that he did, in a way which you have heard from the witnesses and I need not repeat.

The witnesses for the prosecution have said 'clearly a pretext'. You heard Miss Sutton deal with those points just a very short time ago and I won't repeat them. But you may think certainly, very likely, very probably, the whole of this pre-contract matter was a pretext, but, in any event, it didn't in fact matter, because they still remained a danger to Richard, a focal point that those that wished to remove him from the throne, the unpopular Northerner, could have centred round in order to re-establish them. And the fact that they'd been bastardised really didn't matter because if that happened the next claimant to the throne, or the Protector on behalf of Edward V, if he was ever put back there, would have got his parliament to reverse the bastardisation in exactly the same way as Henry VII did when he finally defeated Richard after the Battle of Bosworth. And, therefore, they still were a danger and you may think, therefore, had to be destroyed. And destroyed they were.

Rumour and record at the time, and afterwards, condemned Richard. And you can criticize each one of the Chronicles for some reason or other but, taken as a whole you may think there is every indication in them that Richard was the person who had instigated those deaths. Mancini, from the small excerpts to which you have heard referred, obviously thought that he had done it but effectively says, reading between the lines, 'Well, it doesn't surprise me because of the ruthless disposal of Hastings, but I really don't know and therefore I'm not prepared to say'. He, Mancini, of course, having left London very shortly after the Coronation and therefore not in a position to remain behind to make any further enquiries. Croyland, no positive evidence, the careful insider-historian, who finds it difficult to remain silent altogether and introduces it at least in those verses. Philippe de Commynes, the Frenchman, says it categorically and the other Frenchman, the French Chancellor, makes that public and damning statement. But from Richard, answer comes there not. Silence. Silence resonant in its significance.

Well, members of the jury, do we really need the Tudor historians, I won't call them chroniclers, the Tudor historians at all? More and Vergil? According to Mr Richards, the first Prosecution witness, no. Maybe they are tainted with the Tudor brush and will pervert themselves into writing inaccuracies to ingratiate themselves with the new Tudor King who incidentally was really prepared to let the matter drop, other than in the words of Richard's attainder, in which as Mr Potter has just reminded you, he refers to the 'shedding of the blood of infants'. It's for you to say how much reliance can be placed upon More. Is it the work of an intellectual joker to which no regard should be paid at all? Or is it, as Mr Starkey said, for the reasons which he gave, a record to accept in outline if not in detail? Is no reliance at all to be placed on Polydore Vergil who gives the More version but in less detail, simply because he was commissioned by a Tudor King to write a history of England? And there are the other, later records about which you heard. The defence are forced to say here, well, whenever a chronicler says something which is contrary to Richard's cause they are unreliable or they are Tudor tainted. Members of the jury, it's for you to say. The defence effectively are saying here well, Richard may not have done it. It certainly hasn't been proved that he did. Well members of the jury, you're not being asked to say that you are satisfied so that you are certain that he did, you're only being asked to say that he probably did it. And members of the jury, the defence also seek really, simply to put a different interpretation on the facts.

In the end, as I've said, it comes to this: the Princes disappeared. There were rumours that they were killed, which turned out to be true, you may think beyond any doubt at all. Richard must have known that they were killed and either he had ordered it or he would have been told about it. Brackenbury, the Keeper of the Tower was put there by Richard, a friend of Richard's, and there is no way Buckingham or anybody could have entered that Tower and killed those boys without Brackenbury the Keeper knowing. And Richard would have been the first person to know after that. But what did he do? Absolutely nothing. And that can only mean, we would suggest, as you've heard from Mr Pollard and from Mr Richards, that can only mean that he ordered those executions because otherwise he must have accused the wrong doer to clear himself. And it's no good saying, we suggest, that, well, it could have been somebody else like Buckingham and Richard couldn't do anything about it for fear he wouldn't be believed. He would have been no worse off and certainly probably very much better off to have taken the action of accusation and denial.

Members of the jury, there it is. There's really only one question that you've got to ask yourself: has it been shown to our satisfaction that King Richard probably ordered the deaths of the Princes? If the answer is yes, then he is guilty and we would respectfully submit that the verdict is well-founded upon the evidence which you have heard.

JUDGE: Yes, Mr Dillon.

MR DILLON: May it please Your Lordship.

I too, members of the jury, will be short. You've heard the whole of the evidence which we have been able to compress into this very short period of time and it will have given you a view. Whether you feel that it can possibly have given you a complete view, let alone a complete understanding of the complex problem which you are called upon to consider, may be a very different kettle of fish. Particularly bearing in mind that although we're examining it here in the year 1984, we cannot any of us possibly know what the year 1985 or '6 or '7 may add to our knowledge and understanding of the events that we examine. My Lord, when he began, told you that this question, whether King Richard was the author of, or responsible for, the deaths of the Princes, has been the subject of fierce controversy for five hundred years. It's unlikely that anything that we can do here today is going to resolve that fierce controversy. We can therefore expect books like Mr Potter's 'Good King Richard' next year, to be followed, if not in the same year certainly in the year after, by one describing Richard as a tyrant, with some new view being placed on events, the fringes of which you and I have been able to examine.

We've got to examine these facts, as far as we can, dispassionately, being very careful about over-emphatic and over-positive assertions. Whether you criticise any of my witnesses for being over-positive will be a matter, of course, for your good judgement. You may think that Dr Pollard was somewhat over-positive on the pre-contract and Dr Starkey over-positive on just about everything and so let's be careful, shall we? Knowing that the subject is one which is coloured by emotion and has been distorted by outrages of this kind* and the depiction of Richard III – but this is, I say not in a critical sense of a great actor, you will understand, but that which is imprinted upon all our memories I think – Sir Laurence Olivier in Shakespeare's Richard III.

Let's therefore look at Richard before the death of Edward IV because one cannot ignore the reputation that he had. He is criticised by Mr Richards for having acquired or disposed of some land

* Mr Dillon is gesturing at this point with a copy of the Society of Antiquaries portrait known as Richard with a Broken Sword.

previously belonging to the Warwicks. The carving of great estates was almost a pastime of the rich man during that period, quite apart from other events. He is described as being a man of piety, a man of unswerving loyalty to his brother Edward IV, refusing to divert himself from selfless service for his brother and his brother's family, despite for instance, the treason of Clarence against his brother. A man also who established in the North something which came to be known as the Council of the North within his own Dukedom, justice being made available for all men. It is noticeable that when he was upon the throne his legislation carries that forward as Miss Sutton very briefly indicated to you, I cutting her short in the detail that she could give about that. A King who immediately takes action, as he has as a commoner, in favour of the ordinary person, who then slays those very children especially put into his care. Who says so? Let's examine the commentators upon whom my friend relies.

Commynes, the Frenchman, and I'm not here to denigrate all Frenchmen it will be understood, particularly in today's climate, Commynes, please remember, had perhaps that engaging unreliability which one attaches to the French sometimes. In one part of his history saying it was Richard who slew the children and in another part, the Duke of Buckingham. Does that advance our knowledge? That gentleman living at a distance away from our shore, quite apart from the other considerations that one would have. Take the French Guillaume in January 1484 making his declaration to the States General, in the context of a political speech, advising those listening to him not to give power to the people, that very element that the French people stole from them, for themselves in the French Revolution. He was using – and inaccurately using, because he claimed in the speech that the crowning came after the killing – that perfidious English example in order to teach his particular audience a lesson. It is not a reliable source upon which you and I can firmly grasp and rely.

Then take the two, because I will leave More till last, upon whom my friend does rely, particularly Mancini and Croyland. The prejudice exhibited by Croyland is well enough summarised, Mr Richards was kind enough to agree with me, in that very short passage (there are many others) which I read from the Continuation for which the unknown author was responsible: 'the north whence ever evil takes its rise'. Mr Potter is surely right: they were regarded by the southerner as being dangerous and savage beasts. In the same way that the northerner regarded the south as devious, and slippery, and not to be trusted. Maybe we have to say to ourselves, they were right so to regard the south at that time. Richard was a man unpractised at the Court, he confined his activities to governing and well governing the north. Is Croyland, with that immense prejudice, to be relied upon? Very well, then let me remind you that this man, at the centre of affairs, does not say Richard slew those children. Rumour has it that they were put to death, but no-one knows how. I paraphrase slightly but not inaccurately. Where is the support then, that Richard was guilty of the crime of murder from Croyland? Croyland does not hesitate to point out Richard's responsibility in regard to the death of Rivers and the others in the north, once they had been seized at Stony Stratford, nor does he hesitate to point out Richard's complicity in relation to Hastings, expressing it with all that force and loathing of the southerner for the northerner.

Then let's turn to Mancini, described by the witnesses as an Italian spy with not good English. Let us accept that that is so. With access obviously not to Richard's Court, as I think it was Dr Pollard made clear for us, and some access to Edward's clearly. But access to the southern view, not to the northern view, and our investigation is bedevilled as Dr Pollard agreed, in this sense – that we have nobody upon whom we are able to rely, save a few scattered remnants of Richard's own letters. There is no northern chronicler to put the other view.

Does More put the other view? Not on your life. Remember please, he began his work in 1513; by the time he'd got to Tyrell's confession; of which there is no trace whatsoever, as Dr Starkey was right to point out to me, we have got to 1521. So we are – your arithmetic will be better than mine, seventeen years before the turn of the century, twenty one thereafter – thirty eight years later. More was a boy of four years of age at the time of Bosworth. What kind of reliable account can he give then of those events all those years ago, save a hearsay one, drawn from those forces who were triumphant, the Tudor ones. And who, so soon as Henry Tudor had conquered at Bosworth, like John Rous, were busy with paste, scissors and water, stitching history together again in the way that they wanted it to be read.

We lack information quite clearly, that will be as obvious to you as it is to us this side of the court. We lack, alas, positive concrete information even about the bones. It is appalling to think that we have to learn from Dr Ross that Professor Wright's examination in 1933, upon which historians relied so completely until 1955 when Professor

Ross* made his own enquiries about it, is inaccurate. For there is in truth no blood upon the jaw of the elder child, and even if there were it does not support medically the conclusion that that child suffocated. Was Professor Wright so misled by the old traditional account of More as to distort that view which should have been a purely scientific one? If now today those bones could be exhumed again, those teeth particularly, scientific methods exist which will allow us much more clearly to determine the age and possibly even the dating. The sexing we will never ever be able to deal with, for the children were killed before puberty. Two views, I suggested to you in opening, can validly be taken upon the basis that researches are not yet complete. We must be cautious, you and I, in the approach that we make.

Bear that in mind then, when I talk to you about Buckingham. Mr Potter made it absolutely clear, I hope, to you that he is not giving evidence in saying that Buckingham did it. But consider these facts and ask yourselves whether it is not perfectly possible that Buckingham did in fact take the step which, whether it assisted Richard or not, most certainly would have advanced his own claim to the throne. He had that good claim provided the princes were out of the way. He coveted the throne and he had the opportunity to, as Constable of England, that senior position, to get into the Tower, if not himself, then through agents employed by himself, to kill the Princes.

How does it come about that the chroniclers agree – not Mancini because he had by this time returned to his French master and no doubt busy upon writing the book which was not discovered in Lille library, of all extraordinary places, in 1934 – but Croyland, More and Vergil. And More perhaps was right to know, since he was brought up as a child by Morton, that – what was the word? – 'party intriguer', one of the few in that century who died safe in his bed at a ripe old age. So More might have known that, as soon as Buckingham arrived at Brecon, where Morton was imprisoned on the orders of Richard, so that he had no cause to love Richard, and the two plot. What is it they are plotting? They are plotting that Henry VII should ascend the throne and marry Elizabeth Woodville, the eldest daughter of Edward IV, in order to give extra respectability once he has ascended the throne. That plot could not have taken place unless, you may think,

* It was Paul Murray Kendall who undertook his biography of Richard III in the 1950s. Professor Ross's book was not published until 1981.

Morton and Buckingham were secure in the knowledge that the Princes were already dead.

Why was it, can I pose for you the question, that there was no enquiry as to the fate of the Princes when Henry VII had ascended the throne? Bear with me, would you, for one moment? If Henry wishes to complete the devastation of Richard as a political figure, as a memory in people's minds, if he wished to secure himself against pretenders, show himself to be the avenger of the death of those children, then the first thing that he would have done would be to go to the Tower and make enquiry. The evidence is, and we can only act upon such evidence as is available, that he did nothing of the kind. Is that because if he had done so he would have revealed perhaps that Buckingham was soley responsible for bringing about the death of those Princes? If he established that, then he would have made a bid for the throne of England in conjunction, in the abortive rising late in '83, in conjunction with the man who had put to death the two Princes who stood in his, Henry VII's, way to the throne and that he could not afford to do, for it would not have made his position upon the throne more secure, and so he avoided it.

Why is it, you will ask yourself, that the Queen released the daughters, albeit the pressure upon her that Mr Russell has referred to. But she not only released the daughters, she released the eldest daughter, who was a walking threat to Richard because of the promise of marriage made by Henry VII at the High Altar of Rennes at Christmas '83. And not only did she release the daughters but she sent for her son Dorset. To put him too into the hands and at the mercy of the man whom she knew or believed had murdered her two children, Edward and Richard? Or was it that she knew and believed, or believed, that in fact it was Buckingham who had taken that step, or some person other than Richard?

One other matter, can I refer you to? In relation to the pre-contract. There's nothing that small-minded lawyers enjoy more than anything else, is having a good old fight about a knotty problem about a pre-contract or something of that kind and my learned friend Mr Russell and I, with the assistance of My Lord, could have spent some hours going into the to's and fro's and the pros and cons of this question. I suggest to you, for your consideration, that Miss Sutton's view is a totally valid one, because it is supported by one really remarkable and outstanding fact. That is that while complaint is made, in particular by Dr Pollard, that no examination was made of Bishop Stillington in public about the existence of the pre-contract, the man who had the opportunity of making that examination frustrated the judges of the Exchequer and the Lords in Parliament who had resolved that such an examination of Stillington should take place. The man who prevented that was Henry VII. Why did he do that? If that had revealed, of course, that the two Princes, Edward and Richard, were in fact, bastards, it would have revealed also that his wife Elizabeth was illegitimate and that would not have assisted the security of his seat upon the throne of England.

And so there are layers and layers and layers which have got to be stripped from these facts before one can, in fact, get down to drawing fundamentally important conclusions about the facts which you have examined. Richard's silence can be attributed, certainly in the way that my learned friend Mr Russell has attributed it, to the complicity of Richard. But that is not the only view. Richard would know perfectly well, such was the climate in England at that time, that for him to simply deny the murder of the Princes would not have been acceptable to half the audience to whom he was speaking. So better to remain silent, as he did. It is not one of those facts that one can take hold of as one can a book or a pen and say I have this, I see it, I know it, it proves itself. And there is in the examination that you've got to make here, no one fact which can perform that task for you. For the basic premise of the prosecution case is this: the Princes were a threat; they were in line for the throne and therefore he had to kill them. There was another nephew who was equally a threat if the Princes were in fact a threat. Who was nurtured and harboured by Richard as lovingly as if he was his own son, who so tragically died in the Spring of 1484. Does that not on its own, quite apart from those elements that I have referred to, show you quite clearly that even upon the balance of probabilities, one cannot grasp firmly to say Richard is guilty. We can't prove that he is not. But that is not our task, as My Lord will tell you, for it must be, under our system, the case that the prosecution proves to your satisfaction that Richard is guilty. I thank you for your attention deeply.

JUDGE: Members of the jury, at the beginning of these proceedings – it seems a very long time ago now – I ventured to say that what you, as the sole judges of the facts, are concerned with today is an endeavour to pass a historical judgement on whether King Richard III murdered or caused to be murdered the Princes in the Tower. It is a grave allegation. The fact that the king is dead does not make it less grave so far as his reputation is concerned. Calumnies against the dead, false accusations against the dead, even in a historical inquest, there should not be. If guilt can be established it is for the prosecution to establish it. As Mr Dillon has pointed out to you, it is not for the defence to establish the king's innocence. On the other hand, if the king's guilt is in your view established, then it is right that, at the bar of history, that judgment should stand. For a duty is owed also to the dead Princes is it not? It was the great historian Lord Acton who said, 'History is a judgment seat'. If it can be established the truth should prevail.

At this point of time, when all the potential witnesses are dead, and the documentary evidence available is limited, and to some extent contradictory, certainty in the case there cannot be. This has emerged very clearly, you may think, in the evidence that you have heard from the distinguished historians and experts in the witness box. What view you take of the evidence of the one or the other, and which you believe is entirely a matter for you. You may think that a willingness by a witness to concede the possibility that an opinion may conceivably be wrong, or could reasonably be qualified, is a point more to the credit of the witness than the contrary. But that is a matter for you to decide.

All I wish to say to you at this stage about the broad nature of your duty is this: for the purposes of these proceedings, if, when you consider your verdict, you can conclude and can say that it is more probable that King Richard did murder the Princes than not, then a verdict of guilty would be right. If, on the other hand, the probabilities point to his innocence, or you think that the probabilities are equally balanced, then your verdict should be one of not guilty. You will not forget that you are considering an allegation of murder; the more serious the allegation, the higher the degree of probability that is required.

Now members of the jury, I am not going to review the whole of the evidence. You have heard it and you have been listening carefully to it. The prosecution case has been put frankly as relying on circumstantial evidence. It is based on this broad proposition: the Princes were locked up in the Tower of London when they were under King Richard's protection. They were never seen alive again. They were never seen to leave the Tower of London alive. They could not have

Lord Elwyn-Jones

been spirited away, it is said, or been taken to some other country, without this coming to light at the time. The conclusion that the prosecution invite you to draw is that they never left the Tower, and that they were murdered by the person who had the fullest control and power over them, namely King Richard III.

On this matter you have heard the evidence of the remarkable discovery in the reign of King Charles II of the bones of two young children at the foot of a stair in the Tower of London. On that you have heard the cautious evidence of the witnesses. Doctor Ross concluded that the bones were consistent with being those of the Princes and that possibly they were. The evidence is not conclusive. It was pointed out that the bones certainly did not disclose the cause of death. The suggestion that there was blood stain on the bones or bone and that that was a pointer to suffocation was rejected. The evidence for the defence upon that issue, you have heard and you will bear it in mind.

So members of the jury, it is for you to decide whether the evidence is so uncertain and unsure that you ought to reject it. You may think however, that it is indeed a very remarkable coincidence that there should be found in a box at the foot of the stairs near where the Princes were housed, the bones of two children of at any rate approximately the same age as the Princes. If you accept that evidence, then you may think that the long arm of coincidence has stretched very far if they were not the bones of the Princes in the Tower. But that is a matter for your judgment.

Now the evidence as to what occurred in these proceedings is largely the evidence of contemporary chroniclers and historians. At this hour, I need not retraverse – it will be fresh in your mind.

Emphasis is placed by the prosecution on the fact that King Richard had a powerful motive for killing the Princes. They were potential claimants to the throne. It is said that the fact that their bastardy had been pronounced did not eliminate this danger. It is said that so long as they lived, they remained a challenge and a threat to the King. They were violent days. Killing or threats to kill the occupier of the throne, were part of a recurring pattern at that turbulent time in our island history. The evidence as to potential motive is something that it is proper for you to consider.

Members of the jury there is no direct evidence before you, you may think, of precisely how the Princes died. The history, as written by Thomas More, has not been presented as proof.

You can, of course, have a conviction for murder without being able to establish the existence of the dead body of the victim. If the circumstantial evidence in this case is so powerful that you feel right to accept it as proof of the killing of the victim, and if in this case you conclude there is a high probability that it was the King who did it then you can so find.

On the issue of the claim of the King to the throne, it is suggested by the prosecution that it was bogus and that the story of the alleged bastardy of the Princes was a built-up story to bolster that claim. It is for you to form your own view about that. One of the witnesses for the defence said it was the very crux of the case to establish the bastardy of the Princes because Richard III, it is said, had an undoubtedly good title to which it was proper for him to give effect. It was not a usurpation of power on his part when he became King, but a legitimate claim that he asserted.

Now members of the jury, you may think that a somewhat shadowy figure has appeared in the case namely Buckingham of whom it is said that he might well have been the man who murdered the Princes. If that is so you may think it is surprising that no knowledge of that fact came to, to the ear of King Richard III. Brackenbury the Constable of the Tower was his friend and a close associate of King Richard. You may think that if in fact Buckingham had murdered the Princes, King Richard would not have failed to make that clear and to announce the fact.

What is said by way of criticism of King Richard is that, while the rumour was common that the Princes had been killed, not a word came by way of denial from King Richard that he had done it. Not a word, not a word – although apparently he was quick to deny some other allegation that he was about to marry his neice. Well that is a matter for you to consider. It is said on the King's behalf that he was entitled to reject the charge as grotesque. It was below his standing as a king to deny it. That, members of the jury, is a matter for you.

What has emerged as an interesting feature of the evidence in the case, is the undoubted change in the attitude of chroniclers and even artists to this great question of King Richard's guilt or innocence after the coming of Henry VII to the throne of England. You have heard evidence of the actual distortion of the King's contemporary portraits, if you accept the evidence that this took place. Indeed it has been submitted to you on behalf of the defence that Richard's supposed guilt is almost entirely the product of a Tudor propaganda campaign to blacken his name. You have heard some of the Tudor evidence which is highly critical of King Richard III. But the contemporary evidence arising during his lifetime you may think is more disposed to create at any rate uncertainty as to the perpetrator of the crime.

Well now members of the jury, the time is late and I don't know that I can take the matter further. I now invite you to retire to consider your verdict. There are two verdicts open to you: either a verdict of guilty or a verdict of not guilty. If you find yourselves unable to reach unanimity about your verdict then I will be prepared to accept a majority verdict. I hope that is clear to you. So will you now please be good enough to retire to consider your verdict.

Thank you.

CLERK OF THE COURT: The court will rise.

CLERK OF THE COURT: Be upstanding. Have you reached a verdict on which you are all agreed.

FOREMAN: Yes.

CLERK OF THE COURT: Do you find the defendant guilty or not guilty.

In the interests of allowing you the reader to reach your own decision, as one of the much wider public before whom King Richard stands indicted, the jury's verdict is printed on page 160 together with some brief notes on the jury's reasons for reaching their conclusion.

JUDGE: Members of the jury, if I may address you for the last time . . . Your verdict will I suspect stimulate rather than terminate the controversy that has surrounded the deaths of the Princes. King Richard III has not been allowed to rest in peace. You may assume that the controversy about him will continue as long as interest in our island history continues. And long may that continue. Thank you very much.

CLERK OF THE COURT: The court will rise.

THE
VERDICT
(overleaf)

HOW THE JURY REACHED ITS VERDICT

REACTION TO THE WITNESSES

Mr Richards. A traditional historical statement of events, but without strong expression of belief in Richard's guilt.

Dr Ross. Evidence about bones in the Tower inconclusive. More credence given to incompatability in ages as indicated by bones than to compatability as indicated by teeth.

Dr Pollard. Noted Mancini could not make categorical statement re. Richard's guilt. Mancini, as an Italian without much knowledge of English, was considered unreliable. Pre-contract seen as decisive area of debate. Little doubt cast upon marriage of Edward IV and Eleanor Butler. Lack of satisfactory link between Richard and bastardy story.

Dr Starkey. Encouraged 'to shoot from the hip' by defence barrister, and dynamics of confrontation overshadowed his evidence; the later historians figured little in jury's calculations.

Lady Wedgwood. Made considerable impact, in casting further doubt on the preconceived 'black' image of Richard.

Miss Sutton. Undermined contention that Richard III had motive for killing Princes. Satisfied jury on: marriage of Eleanor Butler and Edward IV; Richard's consequent legal and moral justification in taking throne; his lack of motive for murder on grounds that Princes were bastards.

Mr Potter. Established favourable impression of Richard's character: general conduct appeared reasonably decent and honest; impressive loyalty to brother; quality of rule; no evidence of hatred in south; not at all the evil and unpopular tyrant. Suggestion of Duke of Buckingham's guilt did not weigh heavily but reinforced doubt re. that of Richard, as did Henry VII's failure to investigate the murder. Elizabeth Woodville's apparent reconciliation with Richard suggested she believed him innocent.

FACTORS IN FAVOUR OF THE PROSECUTION

(1) Throne gave Richard strong motive to dispose of Princes. **(2)** Way in which he murdered Hastings showed preparedness to be ruthless. **(3)** Impossible for anyone who was not a close associate of Richard's to have killed Princes as they were being kept in the Tower. **(4)** Richard should bear some of responsibility for deaths as he placed Edward in the Tower and took Richard from sanctuary to· be with him.

FACTORS IN FAVOUR OF THE DEFENCE

(1) Princes might easily have been killed without Richard's knowledge or approval. **(2)** Lack of direct accusation. **(3)** Richard's general conduct. **(4)** Edward's pre-contract of marriage to Eleanor Butler. **(5)** Lack of enquiry by Henry Tudor. **(6)** General feeling that information about Richard was distorted or biased.

CONCLUSION

It was explained that though they the jury understood that they were being asked to come to their decision on a balance of probability, when dealing with a charge as serious as murder it was inevitable that the normal burden of proof, beyond reasonable doubt, should influence their thinking. It was recalled that the jury felt an enormous sense of responsibility about their task and quickly forgot that they were taking part in a paper trial.

POSTSCRIPT

THE BONES OF 1674

As Lord Elwyn Jones predicted, the controversy concerning Richard III and the death of his two nephews has continued to excite public interest. In May 1987 a physical anthropologist from the Natural History Museum published an article which provoked *The Times* to announce 'Modern Science Convicts Richard III' – an assertion which produced an angry response from Richard's defenders.

Dr Theya Molleson[1] cautiously offered support to the attribution that the bones found in the Tower were those of the young Princes Edward and Richard. She developed the comparison made by Dr Jean Ross in *The Trial of Richard III* between the remains of Lady Anne Mowbray, Richard of York's child bride, and those of the two children found in the Tower and now in Westminster Abbey. Anne Mowbray was a distant relative of the princes, and had lain undisturbed in her lead coffin since her death in 1481 at the age of 8 years 11 months. The paper referred not only to the study made of Lady Anne's teeth, but also the examination of her bones which was published in the *London Archaeologist* in 1986,[2] some twenty years after she had been exhumed and re-buried in 1965.

Whilst warning that sex determination in juveniles is 'notoriously unreliable', Dr Molleson states that the remains in the Tower appeared to be those of two males. In the younger child the roots of the incisor and the first molar teeth were complete, but the canine tooth was not ready to erupt, whereas in girls as a rule the canines erupt just after the roots of the other teeth are complete. Turning to the older child, by the

---

1. T. Molleson, 'Anne Mowbray and the Princes in the Tower: a study in identity', *London Archaeologist* 5, no 10 (1987), 258–62.
2. R. Warwick 'Anne Mowbray: the skeletal remains of a medieval child' *London Archaeologist* 5, no 7 (1986), 176–9.

onset of puberty in girls most of the teeth and the ends of the long bones in the wrists and hands have fused together, but in this child, though the teeth had come through, the bones were still not fully ossified. Ricardian critics dismiss[3] the whole basis of Dr Molleson's gender analysis which they say is corrupted by the inadequacies of the original examination in 1933.[4]

Like Dr Ross, Dr Molleson found dental evidence that the two children were related. Both children had hypodontia or missing teeth, a condition so rare that it affects just 3.1 per cent of males and 5.7 per cent of females. A relative of someone with hypodontia is eight times more likely to have missing teeth than a member of the general population. Dr Molleson also noted that Anne Mowbray was related to the Princes. She too had six permanently missing teeth, which could indicate that she was related to the children found in the Tower of London, and by implication this could be taken as further evidence that the bodies found in the Tower are those of the princes.

Richard's defenders have taken issue with this evidence. They argue that at least one of the younger child's teeth could have originally been present and then lost at a very early age; that the combination of missing teeth is the least rare; and that the categories of teeth missing from Lady Anne Mowbray are different to those missing from the Princes. Dr Molleson's own rejoinder is that hypodontia does run in families and appears as a general tendency to have missing teeth, rather than teeth of the same category.

Like Dr Ross, Dr Molleson found the Wormian bones, the distinct bone formations in the skulls of both the Tower children, as further evidence that they might be related. But the Ricardian critics respond that as many as one in two of ancient populations had Wormian bones, and that they have no real significance. Dr Molleson in return emphasises that it is the unusually large size of the bones and the similarity in their shape which she takes as evidence of a blood relationship.

Anthropologists have found that the age of a juvenile is best determined by the study of the development of the teeth rather than the bones. Anne Mowbray's bones lagged 2½ years behind those of a

---

3. P.W. Hammond and W.J. White, 'The Sons of Edward IV', *Richard III: Loyalty, Lordship and the Law*, ed P.W. Hammond, (Yorkist History Trust, London 1986), 104–47.
4. L.E. Tanner and W. Wright, 'Recent investigations regarding the fate of the Princes in the Tower', *Archaeologia* 34 (1934), 1–26.

modern child's, while her teeth were at the stage expected in a twentieth century child of her age at death, which was eight years and eleven months. Using standard techniques, Dr Molleson calculated that Anne Mowbray had a dental age of 8.4 years, yielding a chronological age of between 7.7 and 9.2 years. Using the same techinque the older of the two Tower children came out with a dental age of 14.4 years and a chronological age of between 12.9 and 16 years. Edward V would have been 13 in November 1483. The younger child came out with a dental age of 9.6, giving a chronological age of between 8.6 and 10.7 years. There is some doubt about the precise date of Richard's birth, but he would probably have been 10 in August 1483. In other words, the age of the Tower children was consistent with that of the Princes in 1483/4. Turning to the bones, Dr Molleson took into account the 2½ to 3½ year lag in development observed in Anne Mowbray, and calculated from the Tower children's bones that they were 11½ to 12½, and 13½ to 14½ years old. If the teeth are the most reliable indicator of age, then the younger one was very tall. Dr Molleson noted that the Princes' father Edward IV was known to be 6ft. 3½in., exceptionally tall for that period, but her critics have called this element of her case 'uncomfortable'.

In Dr Molleson's opinion, if the bones are really those of the Princes, then the date of death which is most consistent with the dental and skeletal ages was some time in 1484. It is notable that most contemporary accounts (Mancini, the *Croyland Chronicle*, de Rochefort's speech to the Estates General, the *Historical Notes of a London Citizen*) report the rumours of the Princes' deaths as having occurred in the second half of 1483.

Critics of the bones have little argument with the evidence that makes them consistent with the ages of the Princes in 1483/4, though they raise a question mark about the underdeveloped sacrum of the older child, which Dr Molleson ascribes to spina bifida. However, they feel that the starting point for the whole inquiry is false as the bones could have come from anytime from the Roman occupation to when they were found in 1674. They insist that only carbon 14 dating can decide if the bones even come from the right century; they also urge further examination and chemical testing to try to determine the sex, and whether the two children shared the same blood group. These tests of course may settle nothing. The margin of error with the carbon 14 dating could be a century each way, the tell-tale signs of gender could be missing or contradictory, new chemicals may have contaminated the bones and the significant ones been washed away.

Finally can the bones, tantalising though they may be, ever really prove Richard's guilt or innocence? If the bones are shown beyond a doubt to be those of the Princes, strong circumstantial evidence though it may be, it would not prove, and certainly would not be accepted by his defenders as proof, that Richard was actually responsible. On the other hand evidence that the bones are those of two mere Roman serving lads, would not clear for ever more the name and reputation of King Richard III. In this case it is probably beyond the power of modern science to either convict or acquit.

MARK REDHEAD
July 1987